Chattooga

JOHN LANE

DESCENDING

INTO

THE

MYTH

OF

DELIVERANCE

RIVER

Chattooga

THE UNIVERSITY OF GEORGIA PRESS

Athens & London

Published by the University of Georgia Press

Athens, Georgia 30602

© 2004 by John Lane

All rights reserved

Designed by Kathi Dailey Morgan

Printed and bound by Thomson-Shore

The paper in this book meets the guidelines

for permanence and durability of the Committee

on Production Guidelines for Book Longevity

of the Council on Library Resources.

Printed in the United States of America

08 07 06 05 04 C 5 4 3 2 1

Library of Congress Cataloging-in-Publication Data

Lane, John, 1954–

Chattooga : descending into the myth of

Deliverance river / John Lane.

p. cm.

Includes bibliographical references.

ISBN 0-8203-2611-9 (hardcover : alk. paper)

1. Chattooga River (N.C.-Ga. and S.C.)—History.

2. Chattooga River (N.C.-Ga. and S.C.)—Description

and travel. 3. Dickey, James. Deliverance. 4. Chattooga

River Region (N.C.-Ga. and S.C.)—History.

5. Chattooga River Region (N.C.-Ga. and S.C.)

—Description and travel. 6. Chattooga River Region

(N.C.-Ga. and S.C.)—Biography. 7. Natural history

—Chattooga River Region (N.C.-Ga. and S.C.)

I. Title.   F217.C45L36 2004

917.5—dc22   2003020563

British Library Cataloging-in-Publication Data available

Title page and chapter opener photograph: *Bull Sluice,*
Chattooga River by Jeff Beard

For

Pilley and Payson
Paddlers Past and Present

and

Rob and Russell
Paddlers Present and Future

The river and everything I remembered

about it became a possession to me,

a personal, private possession, as nothing

else in my life ever had. Now it ran

nowhere but in my head, but there

it ran as though immortally. . . .

In me it still is, and will be until I die,

green, rocky, deep, fast, slow, and

beautiful beyond reality.

JAMES DICKEY

Deliverance

CONTENTS

ACKNOWLEDGMENTS

Many thanks to Bill Belleville, Ron Rash, Thorpe Moeckel, Don Greiner, Deno Trakas, Betsy Teter, and Beth Ely, who all read the manuscript at various stages and contributed to shaping this river narrative. And thanks to Esmond Harmsworth, my agent for a brief and shining moment, for guiding the construction of the initial book proposal a few years ago in spite of New York publishing's apathy toward the Chattooga's story. Special thanks go to Wofford College for granting a professional development leave at the beginning of this project, and to the University of Georgia Press and its staff for all its continuing support. And finally, thanks to all who talked to me about the river and paddled it with me over the last twenty years. May we meet again in some eddy above a big Chattooga drop.

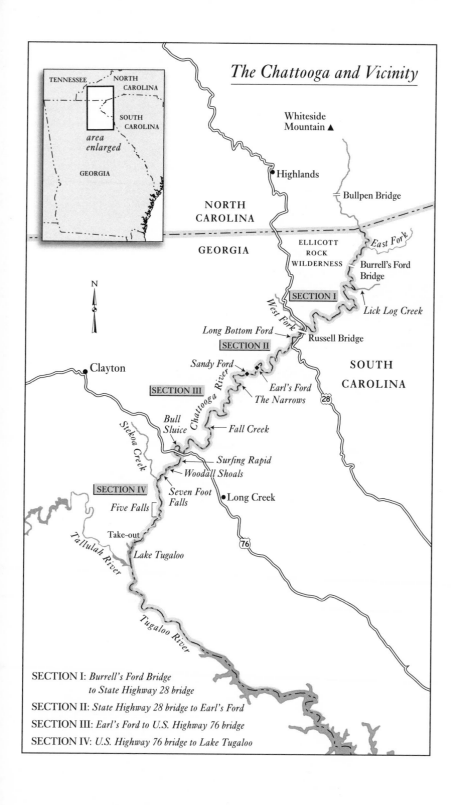

The Chattooga and Vicinity

TENNESSEE | NORTH CAROLINA

SOUTH CAROLINA

area enlarged

GEORGIA

Whiteside Mountain ▲

Highlands

Bullpen Bridge

NORTH CAROLINA

GEORGIA

ELLICOTT ROCK WILDERNESS

East Fork

Burrell's Ford Bridge

SECTION I

Lick Log Creek

West Fork

Long Bottom Ford

SECTION II

Russell Bridge

Clayton

Sandy Ford

SOUTH CAROLINA

SECTION III

Earl's Ford
The Narrows

28

Bull Sluice

Fall Creek

Stekoa Creek

Surfing Rapid

Woodall Shoals

SECTION IV

Seven Foot Falls

Long Creek

Five Falls

Take-out

Tallulah River

Lake Tugaloo

76

Tugaloo River

SECTION I: *Burrell's Ford Bridge to State Highway 28 bridge*

SECTION II: *State Highway 28 bridge to Earl's Ford*

SECTION III: *Earl's Ford to U.S. Highway 76 bridge*

SECTION IV: *U.S. Highway 76 bridge to Lake Tugaloo*

The Myth of the Chattooga

A

PERSONAL

HISTORY

We Southerners are a
mythological people, created
half out of dream, and half
out of slander, who live in
a still legendary land.

JONATHAN DANIELS

A RIVER IS A landscape shaped by powerful and dynamic natural systems, including the human imagination. There's a reason that the flow of a river has been used as a metaphor for life and that of all the landscapes—mountains, oceans, deserts—rivers are what poets and writers return to in literature when describing the way human history cuts across time. The Chattooga River, forming a section of the border between South Carolina and Georgia, has been for me a landscape of discovery. The stories I've heard told about its history, danger, and beauty have shaped my own relationship to rivers.

"I do not know much about gods," T. S. Eliot wrote in *Four Quartets*, "but I think the river is a strong brown god." Eliot grew up along the Mississippi in Saint Louis, the same river Mark Twain used as the backdrop for *The Adventures of Huckleberry Finn* and *Life on the Mississippi,* those classic river texts. What kind of god would Eliot see in the Chattooga, in the shattered blue crystal of a mountain river falling over broken bedrock ledges?

My love of James Dickey's 1970 novel *Deliverance* came before I knew the actual landscape of the Chattooga. The 1972 film, directed by John Boorman and adapted from the novel by Dickey, included river scenes largely shot on the Chattooga, but not exclusively on that waterway. Many of the film's white-water action sequences were shot on Sections III and IV, though the most dramatic scenes featured the waterfalls in the gorge of the nearby Tallulah River.

The novel and film had already been out ten years when in the early eighties, as a beginning white-water kayaker, I encountered the real Chattooga the first time. Nearly twenty years later, in 1999, I began this exploration of the complex relationships the popular imagination creates in the isolated, rugged mountain landscape along the border of Georgia and South Carolina that a *National Geographic* article called "Chattooga Country."

I first read Dickey's novel as a high-school sophomore when it appeared in 1971 as a paperback. I found it compelling, and as a teenager I connected this best-selling adventure novel I read voraciously behind my book in algebra to Joseph Conrad's *Heart of Darkness,* which was assigned in sophomore English. Both were river stories, and both employed a narrator whose world was shaken by what he found upstream.

Dickey imagined a river called the Cahulawassee, based on the remote mountain rivers the poet—a sometime canoeist—had experienced. Dickey's story places four suburban men on a weekend canoe trip down the north Georgia river to face the worst man and nature have to offer. When the story is over, one of Dickey's characters has died, one has been brutally raped, another badly wounded running the rapids, and the final one has returned to tell a tale destined to become one of the central adventure stories of my generation.

Dickey grasped a white-water river's potential as a landscape for heroic action. His poems are full of journeys, and his three novels take a similar shape as well. The poet saw stories as cyclic mythical journeys, rites of passage.

The difference is monumental between what happened to Dickey's four suburbanites "when they decided not to play golf that weekend," as the movie's original trailer teases, and what happened to the 1.2 million paddlers, commercial and private, who have floated the Chattooga since *Deliverance* appeared. In some ways the river has lived up to its hype. Since the movie, over thirty deaths have occurred in the river's formidable white water, and in the years after the movie made the river popular, unpleasant encounters with the locals were not uncommon, though no murders or rapes of "outsiders" were reported.

My encounters with the river have been tame versions of the trip that Lewis Medlock, Ed Gentry, Bobby Trippe, and Drew Ballinger experienced when they left the Atlanta suburbs in Dickey's novel: I load a car with boats and gear, drive from home a few hours to the river, paddle a stretch of it, and head back home. Their story is mythic, a heroes' journey of separation, initiation, and return. Like the old myths, Dickey's fictional journey is a rite of passage for Everyman with a canoe or kayak.

Here, by *myth,* I don't mean the lies people tell about a place, or rumors, legends, or tall tales that develop around a landscape. Myth is part of our unconscious and therefore beyond words. "Myth is metaphor," Joseph Campbell liked to say. His PBS interviews with Bill Moyers, "The Power of Myth," introduced mythology and how myth works in our lives to millions in the 1980s. "A myth doesn't point to a fact; the myth points beyond facts to something that informs the facts," Campbell once said in an interview.

We can approach myth through words—Freud used "slips" of the tongue to locate our unconscious desires—but words can't fully define our myths. Words can only point the way.

The myth of a place like the Chattooga River is what was said before we arrived and what is left unsaid when we leave. Thinking about the Chattooga as myth helps me define the way the landscape works on my insides when I come into contact with the real river and helps me understand what remains with me when I go home. It's like Campbell's idea of a "mythic journey" seen in mythic stories, fairy tales, almost any narrative—separation from home, initiation, return. It's what a mention of the river conjures in many who know it, a certain set of unconscious expectations—the river as a place of great beauty, safety, fear, danger—that are often in conflict with what their senses tell them when they visit it.

"Funny thing about up yonder," Lewis says to Ed as the adventurers speed toward the distant blue mountains and falling rivers in *Deliverance*, "the whole thing's different. I mean the whole way of taking life and the terms you take it on." The terms on which I take the real Chattooga were formed through twenty years of paddling and hiking. It's always seemed an Eden, and yet I realize that to many it's been destroyed by the love of people like me.

Dickey believed that Chattooga country had been destroyed by being discovered, but I don't want to admit that the potential of the place is really less than it was, nor that protection and use in the past thirty years have diminished the worth of the river. "People have loved the river to death," one fisherman told me when I described the exploration I wanted to undertake in the watershed. "I hope you don't plan to add to that."

If the river has been loved to death, the romance started long before the present. Mississippian Native Americans burned and farmed the Chattooga's bottoms for centuries, and when the Cherokee moved on to the same sites, they continued these agricultural practices. Colonial farmers appropriated the Cherokee land, and later loggers dished out lots of hard love in the eighteenth, nineteenth, and twentieth centuries. For the last few decades, the Forest Service has managed the land, and now hundreds of thousands of people escape to Chattooga country for boating, fishing, hiking, and camping. Some in the surrounding rural communities see government management practices as less than ideal. "Look over there," one local resident told me. "With that government corridor they've created a desert, and nobody can make a living there but a bunch of rich kids with colorful boats."

Later in his life, Dickey thought the river had been spoiled because too many people had gained access to it. The Chattooga as wilderness had somehow faded in his imagination. Was he right? I admire Dickey's poetry and novels, but I'm not sure I agree with the dead poet, a man with a documented flair for exaggeration. Dickey was no expert canoeist, though he had canoed some white water in the early sixties with his Atlanta friends Lewis King and Al Braselton. Nor was Dickey a master hunter or bowman, nor an expert at camping or woodcraft.

James Dickey may never have been an adventurer like Lewis Medlock, but he was a writer whose prose and poetry cut quickly and often against the grain of status quo, surface politeness, and boredom. His messy life (and powerful art) showed what Henry Hart, his biographer, calls "the will to kick free from all judicious restraints." Dickey once said, "If your life bores you, risk it." Dickey seemed to really believe that, and he wanted his fiction and poetry to show it.

Dickey paddled the Chattooga only once and saw it only a handful of times, most often during the filming of *Deliverance*. In James Dickey's landscape, the line where fantasy leaves off and his real river experiences begin is hard to discern.

In the mid-eighties I was teaching at the South Carolina Governor's School for the Arts, and Dickey came to visit our poetry class. That night after his reading I cornered him at a party with hopes of hearing some true-life "combat" story from his trips down white-water rivers. I was approaching him as a fellow boater, and I hoped that he could add to the legacy of Chattooga stories I'd been gathering since I started paddling the Wild and Scenic River a year or two before.

When I asked Dickey to tell me about his first trip down the Chattooga, he seemed at a loss. He told a story instead about Burt Reynolds and the terrible time director John Boorman's crew had filming on the river. Dickey didn't talk as if he knew white-water rivers. There were no technical stories of missed eddies in Jawbone or frightening swims over "the single drop" of Bull Sluice at three feet. Dickey was like his character Ed Gentry, who had little experience with a river, but would never forget what he did have, and savored the possibility for deliverance from the day-to-day that such an experience gave "a regular Joe."

In Dickey's work he returned to rivers often, and powerfully, but rather than an approachable landscape, rivers were a blank wilderness screen where the artist could project his rugged vision of a place for what the poet has called "energizing . . . qualities which otherwise would never have a chance to surface." For Dickey, those qualities were often violent and sexual, and it was sometimes through encounters with the locals that he sketched out these fictional impulses. It is in his portrayal of local people, whether it's the "hillbillies" in *Deliverance* or the Japanese later in *To the White Sea,* where Dickey can be most deeply questioned. It's wrong to dismiss the encounters as mere fabrications. "Those people are out there," a long-time resident of the Chattooga watershed said to me once when I suggested naively that Dickey had created stereotypes in Lonny the banjo boy or the Griners or the mountain man who brutally rapes the outsider from Atlanta. "They're just not the *only* people out there."

From Dickey I have not learned much about my own obsessions or fears, but I see his obsessions and fears in many of the people I encounter on rivers. I go to the river if I want to know about the Chattooga. I pull down Dickey's work if I want to understand more deeply the desires and fears of unprepared characters when they come into contact with people and places they don't really understand.

But do we really fully understand any place? Can I criticize Dickey for not knowing the Chattooga in some profound way, when all my trips into the watershed have added up to less than a year's presence?

For those like the fictional Lewis who resist restraint, Dickey might be right about the way the Chattooga has changed. Today, Lewis would be chased down by the Forest Service for speeding up a country road trying to find the river. Permits are not required for hiking, but they are for camping in the national forest anywhere outside the Ellicott Rock Wilderness or the Wild and Scenic River corridor. If you are in these areas you are not allowed to camp any closer than fifty feet from the river. All boaters must fill out permits at their put-in points. All this regulation might make for a very tame wilderness, a place where it's no longer possible to experience life without restraint. If there's any wildness left in the Chattooga watershed, there's no doubt where it's found—not on the government-maintained trails through the federal wilderness, but in the water itself, running wild and free over resistant rock. It is there—in the ceaseless flow, the curling current—that Lewis could still find his wildness.

In *Deliverance* James Dickey describes the current in a white-water river "like a thing made of many threads being pulled." On the Chattooga the threads of human and natural history have become increasingly tangled and may never be untangled again. "The Chattooga, where we did *Deliverance* . . . it's ruined now by people trying to cash in on it," Dickey said in an interview a few years before he died in 1997. "It's screwed up now."

Adventure tourism on the Chattooga has reached levels some consider impossible for maintaining a "wilderness" experience. In 1983, when I first paddled the Chattooga, fifty thousand floated it. In 2001, commercial and private users of the river approached one hundred thousand. The last several years, commercial river use has actually dropped off a little, and a high-profile drowning on Section IV in the late nineties brought the Chattooga's various communities—the environmentalists, the commercial outfitters, the locals, the politicians, the agency charged with management of the river—into visible public conflict.

As the millennium turned, the public's resolve, so clear in the sixties and seventies, to maintain federal wilderness land seemed to be weakening. Though the laws seem safe from repeal, there are current political debates. Under recent administrations, *privatization* has become the watchword for those known as free-market environmentalists, the idea being that private landowners can manage landscapes better than the government. To travel into the Chattooga watershed is to venture into the middle of all these issues.

In spite of these government complications, Dickey's isolated wilderness landscape is a reality. The wild country is still there, lots of it, even though many of the Georgia and South Carolina rivers with Native American names like the Chattooga have now been drowned under power-company lakes. These lakes still have rivers under them that the fictional Lewis could have recognized from his old maps. These rivers are literally dammed, just as the imaginary Cahulawassee was in Dickey's fictional dream. Part of the mystique of the Chattooga is that it is one of the few rivers in the area to survive the demand for electric power and recreation.

Another part of the Chattooga's myth Dickey helped create is that the river can change you, and I have to admit it worked on me. My idea of wildness, natural beauty, and freedom may not be Lewis's, but it is always measured against what I've seen and continue to experience floating the river.

In 1972, when I stood in line with millions of others to absorb Hollywood's mythic images in John Boorman's film of white water, broken boats, and dangerous mountain men, I was impressed by the violent and beautiful river scenes. Because these scenes had been shot nearby, I watched *Deliverance* with a particular interest I didn't have in the settings of other popular films from that period.

Somehow knowing that *Deliverance* was filmed one hundred miles from my high school in upstate South Carolina legitimized my place for me. I found out years later that the novelist Walker Percy articulated this process, saying that movies "certified" a place. The *Deliverance* river was solidly certified, in my mind, by the time I first placed my boat in its current in 1983.

In my dreams I feared who might come out of the woods and what would be beyond the next bend, but in reality by 1983 I had topographical maps, river guides, and the experience of friends to confirm that Dickey's *Deliverance* river only existed on the shelf and on the screen.

Experiencing a real place, it seems logical, would cause the fictional one, the mythical other, to be left behind. With the Chattooga, that does not seem to be the case. The *Deliverance* river still sits atop the real river as an early morning mist sits atop the flowing current.

"One would think—or so we have been taught to imagine—that dreams are fragile things easily destroyed by reality. But increasingly, the opposite is true," Orville Schell wrote of the myth of Shangri-la in *Virtual Tibet*. Schell found that a real place (in his inquiry, Tibet) often is obscured by the dreams—whether the rafter's conquest or the developer's plans—we project upon it. I found the same true of the Chattooga. On the border of Georgia and South Carolina, the dream landscape dies hard.

In Dickey's novel four men are drawn from their safe but circumscribed suburban homes for a weekend of adventure in the north Georgia woods on a river that will soon disappear beneath the waters of a reservoir. Their dream is that they will be somehow delivered from the day-to-day. Their nightmare is that they are.

I can never leave behind Dickey's dark river when I paddle, even though little in my experience suggests I should be afraid of anything in the Wild and Scenic River corridor except a missed roll and a hard swim in the middle of a run of the difficult rapids on Section III or Section IV. But for me, each encounter with the real Chattooga is still informed by the dark, dangerous stream the Dickey novel and Boorman film bring me to expect. Maybe that's because, for me, the place was literature before it was place, or maybe the staying power of *Deliverance* is simply the power of popular culture, the power of myth.

I don't remember feeling like a hero when I first paddled a white-water river, and I certainly didn't have to climb a cliff and kill anyone with a bow and arrow to finish the trip. I do remember a great deal of fear concerning what was around the next bend, though my fear didn't start with the Chattooga.

While I was in college I played around at white-water canoeing the two or three times a friend talked me into going on trips. During my senior year—1977—I went on two canoe weekends in a row, one on the Green River, an energetic stream always popular with summer camps, less than an hour from the college, and the other on the Nantahala River, a legendary white-water run near the Smoky Mountains. It was on these two streams with a group of novice paddlers that I experienced my initiation into white water. I remember nothing noble or mythic about either outing. I went on them the way someone goes to an amusement park. It was, I thought, merely a way to get a safe thrill on a white-water roller coaster.

Other southern colleges with more money and long-standing outing-club traditions—Sewanee and Davidson in particular—used more formal programs to develop paddling skills and appreciation for the outdoors. Though at times Wofford students called their love of white water a club, there was no chartered organization at the school in the seventies. At Wofford, white-water adventure was driven by the personality of psychology professor John Pilley. Short and compact, with close-cropped hair and glasses held in place with an elastic retainer, Pilley is still, thirty years later, a Popeye with gymnast's biceps. Paddling was perfect for him, all upper body, arms and shoulders. We knew, even if we didn't take Pilley's classes, that every weekend he would probably be out exploring the mountains and we were welcome to come along. News about trips circulated freely among the students, but it was understood that the leaders of each trip were responsible for who could go.

Pilley accompanied us on the two canoe trips, though we novices knew he paddled most weekends with another group of hard cores. Blue Hole canoes were available to us because most of these serious boaters, like Pilley and a half-dozen students, had begun to paddle kayaks. Several of these hard-core kayakers floated with us when we ran the Green and the Nantahala. As they drifted along beside us in their red fiberglass kayaks, they had the bored yet knowing countenances of those who have been to battle. They had seen serious white water, their ease seemed to say, and paddling novice streams was merely an amusement, a tune-up.

Six years later I came back to teach at Wofford, and Pilley quickly talked me into slipping on a kayak. My first experiences with the one-person craft weren't much more pleasant than my earlier canoe trips. Pilley says I was a beginner longer than anyone he had ever taught to paddle. I swam every major and minor rapid on all the intermediate rivers in the region—the Green, the Nantahala, the French Broad. It took a year before Pilley agreed I was ready to descend a section of the Chattooga.

By that time, I was prepared. So my first encounter with the Chattooga would have been pure enjoyment if it had been warmer. It was the winter of 1983, two days after Christmas. I was still getting comfortable in a kayak, and so paddling the *Deliverance* river, though not scary, was an event. The conditions were not perfect when we headed for the Chattooga the first time. It had been in the teens the night before, but Pilley assured me the weatherman was predicting a high near fifty for our outing. He said he wanted me to see the river in winter.

Driving over with me from Spartanburg, Pilley told stories about other trips down the river. There were the near misses to recount, or the times when Pilley or one of his old paddling buddies had almost drowned on the flood-stage river. This would become our ritual of preparation over the years. We would relive Dickey's story, minus the terrible consequences. I asked Pilley if he had ever been on the river after any of the white-water deaths, and he told a story about floating with a group down through the Narrows on a Sunday morning and finding the body of a paddler who had died upstream the day before.

Our float proved not to be so dramatic. It was a short one, only the top of Section III, from Earl's Ford to Sandy Ford, a distance of about three miles. Section III is not the most difficult of the Chattooga's four stretches (Section IV downstream of the Highway 76 bridge owns that distinction), but it offers plenty of challenging white water. It was a good place for Pilley to introduce me to the river.

When Pilley and I put in, it was still cold enough to see our breath. We were dressed for it though, not a natural fiber on either of us: polypropylene, nylon paddling jackets, wet-suit booties. It was quiet on the river and very cold, I thought, to be messing about in boats. There was ice in the shallows and the eddies glistened with a crystal sheen. As Pilley and I spun our boats into the first eddies just downstream from the white sand and stream-cobble beach of the Earl's Ford put-in, we cracked through a thin layer of ice. Pilley was an experienced winter paddler so he had brought gloves, a set of ten-year-old neoprene mittens that he had made himself from a pattern he'd found in the back of a scuba-diving magazine. Back when Pilley started to paddle, everything was homemade and durable. I'd forgotten my factory-made modern scuba-diving gloves. When we reached the river from the parking lot, a walk of a quarter mile down through thick winter woods, I nearly borrowed a pair of leather gloves—just something to shield the water a little—from an old man fishing at the put-in. He was carrying a pint of Jack Daniels and seemed in no danger from the cold.

The river had that winter stillness about it. The only life we saw as we paddled down was a pair of mallards in an eddy where the sun was shining. Southern woods in winter are not only silver and dark. There are many conifers along the river—white pines, hemlocks— and the mountain laurel holds its green all winter, though dulled by the cold. It was so cold that the laurel leaves had curled inward like fat fingers around the branching stems. The most noticeable difference in the winter woods was how deep we could see into them. We could make out gray outcrops along the deep cleft of the valley a hundred yards into the forest.

Though not windy, it was cold, too cold for anyone but Pilley and his homemade gloves. My hands cramped gripping the paddle shaft. Pilley, I imagined, had paddled the river under just about all conditions. If the river has a human spirit, it is Pilley, who has paddled here for thirty years. Even back then it looked as if he had almost become the river, his skin gone dark and rugged like the rocks we passed.

Soon after putting on the river, we saw where Warwoman Creek enters the Chattooga from the Georgia side. Warwoman, a Class III rapid, is where beginners usually spill if they aren't ready for what's below. The rapid has two ledges; the first we ran right of center, and the second, a tricky left to right move through rocks. I did fine, following Pilley through and eddying out at the bottom. Sitting in the pool at the rapid's base, Pilley said he's always thought that Warwoman is the first rapid we see the *Deliverance* canoes slip through on Hollywood's river. He said he liked to sit here for a moment and gaze upstream into movie history.

A mile downstream we floated past First Island Rapid, and at two miles, Rock Garden, another rapid featured in *Deliverance*. In Rock Garden the Chattooga's rapids and riverbed began to take on that distinctive undercut intensity *Deliverance*'s director of photography Vilmos Zsigmond exploited so hauntingly. Black spears of broken bedrock, stone fingers pointed upstream. The current took me slowly under one of them, floating me through a portal. In the cold they seemed particularly ghostly, pointing back toward the put-in.

As we passed through Rock Garden, Pilley reminded me that Dick's Creek Ledge, the first more difficult Class IV rapid on Section III, was just below. We scouted the river-wide ledge of rock from the exposed flat section in the center of the river. I looked down and noticed that the lip of the scouting rock was scarred with blue, red, and yellow residue, the history of a dozen years of plastic canoes beaching there.

Pilley pointed below and described how it was best to slip into the S-turn move that drops you six feet into an eddy behind a big rock cushioned by the current at the bottom. He said to follow him. "Avoid going left of the cushion," he said and he slipped into his kayak, popped his spray skirt into place, took several paddle strokes to push himself clear of the rock, and lined up for the descent. Soon he sat waiting in the lower eddy.

I followed, sliding quickly down through the white water, and spun into the eddy, almost flipping at the bottom. That day, the good flow made it a little frightening—current cantilevered, coursing, surging over ledges and into pools. The water was pushy. When my bow reached the eddy, Pilley was there to give me a brace as I tipped toward the cold water. It was over that fast, my first big rapid on the Chattooga. For years I carried a residual Dick's Creek fear with me each time I approached the ledge.

An hour after leaving the put-in, we were just upstream from the narrow run to the right of the island at Sandy Ford, our take-out. By the time we reached the island, the temperature had finally climbed into the high forties, and the sun, a flat winter disc, had barely staggered over Chattooga Ridge. We both became quiet as we approached this final stretch of white water upstream from our take-out. Above the rapid, we pulled into a calm eddy behind a large boulder on the Georgia side. The water level is usually measured in feet from zero (zero being the height of the river surface above a reference elevation) on a white-water river, and on that day it was close to two feet. There had been some soaking winter rains, and no leaves were on the trees to pull the run-off out of the water table. Two feet is a good level for the Chattooga any time of year, but it was particularly exciting in December.

The rapid below us was not that difficult—a Class II on a scale of VI—but the hundred yards of boulders to the right of the island were challenging. It was what paddlers call a rock garden (fast, shallow water with rocks scattered throughout), and we'd have to pick our way down slowly from eddy to eddy. There were at least ten eddies in the hundred yards, and we tried to catch them all. I could see them stretching below us and out of sight where the rapid ended in the wide calm water of Sandy Ford.

Just off my stern, sun-bleached logs had piled up against the leading tip of the island, refuse from years of the storm surge of flood water. The large logs were matted and jumbled like straws. The power of the river is striking, even on calm beautiful December days.

I watched Pilley below me as he sat at the top of the rapid in his old Holloform, the first plastic kayak commercially available. He was pointed upstream toward me, sitting behind a large boulder, hanging in the eddy. I watched as he leaned forward in the kayak and took short, quick strokes, one long sweep, and then peeled out and into the current. Quickly and smoothly, he dropped down to the next eddy, and I followed into the one he had vacated. Pilley sat for a moment surfing a wave just to the right of the rock, then floated down to the next eddy. He repeated, and I followed, all the way to the bottom.

Soon we were through the long shoal and floating past Sandy Ford, where an old road once crossed the river, connecting South Carolina and Georgia. There are good sand beaches there, and in spite of the national laws establishing the Wild and Scenic River, there is still a rough dirt road down to the river's edge on the Georgia side. In the summer, some locals drive their trucks and cars to the edge of the river, pull out their coolers, turn up their stereos, and crank up Hank Williams Jr. They sit belly-deep in the river in collapsible lawn chairs and raise hell. It's always a shock to slip through the broken gneiss of the shoal, wrapped in the kicked-up spray from falling water, and see three or four men in the river hefting Budweisers to the blue sky of the wilderness.

That day we had the Chattooga all to ourselves. Not even the ducks stayed with us. There were only the dark charcoal shadows of the winter trees against the outline of the hills and the green brush strokes of white pines. If it hadn't been so cold, maybe we would have floated the next ten miles to Highway 76, the final bridge of three that cross the river corridor.

"It's a perfect river," Pilley said as we pulled up at the take-out and popped our skirts.

And so twenty years ago I entered the myth of the Chattooga, like Saint George chasing his dragon. I'm not suggesting that now there is a huge billboard along the road every time I drive down to the

Chattooga that says Mythic Landscape Ahead. Most of the river's early paddlers, like Pilley, or Lewis King, Dickey's model for Lewis Medlock, were drawn to the river for its powerful white water and challenge, not its potential to give paddlers a deeper understanding of themselves and their relationship to nature. These early paddlers learned by trial and error, as I did, how to handle the complexities of current and stone. They probably weren't even aware they were caught in the same forces of nature Dickey's characters would grapple with in *Deliverance*. These are the types of relationships to reality that writers consciously work out, not canoe clubs, weekend adventurers, or outfitters.

Not everyone with a stake in the Chattooga visits on day trips the way we boaters most often do. All the years I paddled the Chattooga, I always focused on the river. I never thought much about the people who live nearby, the locals, those a friend calls "the indigenous ones."

River running in the southeast came of age among people like college students and professors, lawyers, and the business class in southern cities. Not often were these early paddlers the farmers, loggers, and small-town merchants who populate the South Carolina, Georgia, and North Carolina counties bordering the Chattooga River. "A *canoe* trip?" one of the Griner brothers says incredulously in *Deliverance* when Lewis asks if he'll take the cars downstream to Oree. I'm not suggesting that the indigenous ones didn't love the Chattooga before the white-water paddlers discovered it, or that they don't love it now. Their love is primal, a part of them. "Something you see every day, you take for granted," one friend explained. "But you'd sure as hell would miss it if it were gone." To locals, the river is often beyond description. To them it's something akin to home, a place you feel your connection to very deeply but cannot articulate. The idea of getting in a boat and floating from one bridge to the next is still something many locals don't think makes much sense. Dickey's character, one of the Griner brothers, says, "I ain't never been down in there much. There ain't nothing to go down there for. Fishing's no good." Today, some of the locals paddle kayaks and rafts, and many even fly-fish in the deep isolated gorges upstream. And some of the paddlers argue that several decades of habitation have established them as locals and that they have the same stake in the river as the indigenous ones.

Early on in my exploration of this subject, one thread led me out of the Chattooga watershed and into North Carolina. Thomas Rain Crowe, a writer in Tuckaseegee, had told me he knew a man who had worked on the movie set. I should go and talk to him, he said. So I drove over the mountain toward Sylva, a small mountain town that had been filmed for one of the final scenes of *Deliverance*. Ken's Grocery, a yellow Shell station and video parlor, was hanging on a narrow strip of land between another mountain river and a state highway. It doubled as a big-game check-in station.

Inside, the store was a modern mountain one-stop: fast food, videos, and hot dogs. Ken Chastain was behind the counter. He was tall, in a pressed short-sleeve, pale-yellow dress shirt. I said I'd heard he had some *Deliverance* stories. He smiled. Thirty years ago he'd helped set the charges for the blast at the dam site the film crew captured for the movie's opening credits.

"Remember that road down to the dam site?" Ken said, laughing. "I drove that road every morning for three years when we were building that dam over the mountain at Jocassee. You know, that's the lake where in the movie the arm raises up at the end."

He introduced Norma, his wife, who was working behind the video counter. "You ever rent it out?" I asked.

Norma squinted hard and said she did, that they keep *Deliverance* in stock and it's rented quite often: "You know Burt was on a talk show once and he said the worst place he ever ate was right down there in Sylva. Old Burt, he came in here and pissed everybody off."

"I saw *Deliverance* when it came out at the Ritz down in Sylva," Ken said. "Some guys had been at the premiere in Atlanta so the word had already come back that it was really down on us. But when they turned it loose at the theaters I went down to see it anyway."

He said a hush fell over the movie house when the "hillbillies" came on the scene.

"You remember it, don't you?" he asked Norma, who nodded.

"It got under people's skin around here," she said, remembering. "That's a fact."

Ken said you could feel the tension in the theater, "especially in that part where they have sex and squeal like a pig."

"To me that movie was making fun of us," Norma said. "You still have people coming in here saying, 'You're not *really* from around here are you?'"

"You could tell they thought they were better than us," Ken said. "They leveled off the top of a damn mountain down there at Jocassee so they could fly in their helicopters up from Atlanta. If they weren't flying, they were driving Scouts and Rovers."

The river, and the people who live around it, are beginning to take on a personality, one my old friend Pilley might not completely recognize. Now the Chattooga comes alive for me not only through my memory of it from river trips but through its human and natural history and the legacy of stories, hundreds of them, told to me by those isolated from it by time or distance and those close enough to see it every day. Norman Maclean ends *A River Runs through It* by saying, "I am haunted by waters." Maclean's book is the story of two brothers, local boys who love to fish and fight, and the Montana mountain river that is the backdrop for their struggles. Dickey was a southerner, and Maclean a westerner. I don't believe Maclean was haunted by the same ghosts James Dickey's characters encounter in the dark forests along the Cahulawassee. Maclean's ghosts were more similar to mine. In his novella, very real people love the river and work up an intimacy with it throughout their lifetimes. My intimacy with the Chattooga has come over time as I've paddled, hiked, and driven through the watershed. Most of my visits have been recreational, though in recent years I have also traveled to the area looking for inspiration and the shadows of Dickey's novel. Intimacy also comes from reading, and I've piled my study high with newspaper and magazine articles, books and newsletters about the river. Spring is a good time to come to the mountains. The water is high and the wildflowers are beginning to bloom. Mountain laurel, tulip poplar, dogwood, and redbud are in complete display. The air is crisp and clear. So in March I pack my truck and begin my search for the real and mythical Chattooga. I know its many ghosts—from memory and imagination—hang hauntingly in the mist.

Headwaters

CASHIERS,

NORTH CAROLINA

A kind of expectation, based

on obvious metaphors, attaches

to sources and headwaters.

FRANKLIN BURROUGHS

The River Home

*I*T'S EARLY March when I drive to the headwaters of the Chattooga. As I climb into the mountains, the still-dormant rhododendron and laurel snarls encroach on the shoulders of narrow South Carolina Highway 107. I look to the left of my speeding truck, through the dark undergrowth, for creeks, the river's advance guard, marching inch by inch back into the ridge. It has rained hard for a day or so, and as the highway swings around swells of native rock, the run-off peels into the Chattooga drainage, burbling through culverts and ping-ponging off stream pebbles weathered from the old Appalachian range.

The blacktop straddles the ridge between the watersheds of the southwesterly flowing Chattooga River and, to the east, the southeasterly flowing Keowee River. Both rivers are part of the upper reaches of the Savannah River drainage. The Savannah is like a pitchfork resting on the coastal plain, piedmont, and mountain front of Georgia and South Carolina. Just up the highway, the pitchfork's prongs will soon poke slightly over the border into North Carolina.

As I drive I am caught in a switchback of expectations. How is it that I know one part of the river well, while another part—these upper reaches, more creek than river—is unknown territory to me? The Chattooga's familiar personality is thirty miles further downstream where the river gathers some size and the well-known white water starts. Down there is the country where the mythic landscape of the Chattooga begins. But this is white-water country too. Gradient, the number of feet per mile a river drops, creates excitement among those who love to paddle kayaks, canoes, and rafts; the drop down on the main sections of the river average seventy feet per mile. Here in steep upper reaches, the Chattooga's gradient reaches two hundred feet per mile. Where the river encounters more resistant rock in its journey, a waterfall forms. Every white-water boater depends on geology the way sailors ride wind and weather.

Destruction of rock—even mountains—is what a river does. Up here in the headwaters of the Chattooga, eighty inches of rain fall a year, plenty of precipitation to charge the two watersheds falling off to my left and right with a formidable flow. These drainage basins are dynamic systems of erosion, transportation, and deposition, as tons of abraded rock and soils are carried downstream toward the Atlantic. Sand on the beach at Tybee Island, downriver from Savannah, Georgia, was once the scenery up here. All around me the little creeks along the edge of the Chattooga's drainage scratch like fingers for the top of the ridge of rock supporting the road. It's taken millions of years, but the river has had its way, even with the mountains.

There's a paradox within the natural processes at work on the sloping ridges all around me. The headwaters area is the initial source of the Chattooga's flow, the place where the water starts its journey to the sea, but it's also a place of present endings, the current limit of the river's headward erosion away from the sea. If there are expectations of the headwaters, they are double-edged. The river's relationship to the land is so much like our relationships with rivers: dynamic and ever changing, a mixture of gain and loss.

Explorers and visitors from the outside like me have always entered these mountains by following rivers and creeks toward their source. Prehistoric and historic Native Americans followed these rivers for thousands of years prior to the arrival of the Europeans. Some settled in the bottoms, where the high mountain gorges opened up and trapped sediment from upstream after spring floods. The Cherokee established a town on the river just upstream from the ford where Highway 28 crosses today. The small settlement was called *Tsatu'gi,* a word said to be of Creek origin meaning either "he drank by sips" or "he has crossed the stream and come out on the other side." It came to be the name of the whole river, Chattooga.

I'm meeting Buzz Williams, the executive director of the Chattooga Conservancy, in Cashiers, North Carolina, for breakfast. Cashiers is a resort town that straddles the ridge at the back wall of the Chattooga drainage. Buzz has suggested we meet in Cashiers because it makes perfect sense: start at the top of the watershed, and "it's all downstream from there."

Buzz knows the river as well as anyone. He's spent two decades chasing down answers to questions about its human history and ecology and since 1995 has shared his findings in the *Chattooga Quarterly,* a newsletter published by his organization. I have faith that Buzz will know how to go directly to the heart of the Chattooga, past all the *Deliverance* mythology. The heart of it, I can see as I drive toward Cashiers, is wildness and beauty.

For thirty years wildness on the Chattooga has depended on the Wild and Scenic Rivers Act, among whose protected rivers the Chattooga was included in 1974. The act is a powerful conservation tool, though one whose impact could be far greater. The United States has 3.5 million miles of rivers and less than 1 percent designated Wild and Scenic by the 1968 act of Congress. The Wild and Scenic Rivers Act specifies which streams qualify. Rivers protected by the act must possess one or more of the set "values." Wild rivers must be free of dams and generally inaccessible except by trail, with watersheds or shorelines essentially primitive and waters unpolluted. These wild rivers should, as the act states, be "vestiges of primitive America." Scenic rivers must also be dam-free, and their shorelines and watersheds must remain largely undeveloped, but they can be accessible in places by roads.

The Chattooga was the first river east of the Mississippi added to the Wild and Scenic River System. Forty of the Chattooga's fifty-seven miles are classified as wild, two miles as scenic, and fifteen miles as recreational. The federal corridor, established to ensure the river remains as undisturbed as possible, comprises fifteen thousand acres extending out one quarter mile from the riverbanks. There are five road crossings along the Chattooga's forty-seven miles, but motorized vehicles aren't allowed within the corridor. There are also strict guidelines for hiking, fishing, camping, and boating.

Along the upper reaches, the river is protected further by the nine thousand–acre Ellicott Rock Wilderness Area. The wilderness is named for Major Andrew Ellicott, a surveyor from Pennsylvania commissioned in the first decade of the nineteenth century to determine the line between Georgia and South Carolina. Ellicott was already a well-known surveyor by the time he hiked into these mountains along the Chattooga. He had previously been a member of teams that worked on extending the Mason-Dixon line and surveying the site of the city of Washington, D.C.

During the centuries of settlement, there was an additional sort of wildness in this area. Georgia and South Carolina had argued over their upper boundary since 1803. The two parties could not agree on the position of the thirty-fifth parallel. In 1804 Georgia's claim on "the Orphan Strip" deteriorated into a near war. In 1809 David B. Mitchell, the governor of Georgia, finally dispatched Ellicott's survey expedition into the mountains. The actual Ellicott rock, set in 1811, is lost, but was located probably somewhere within a few hundred yards of another marker, the Commissioner's Rock, placed in 1813 to clarify the boundary between North Carolina and South Carolina and inscribed "Lat 35 AD 1813 NC + SC." This marker set the location of the thirty-fifth parallel for future generations, settling a frontier and creating for present-day wilderness hikers an ironic goal: find in the mountain laurel along the Chattooga a place marker for political struggle and geographic certainty.

When I arrive in Cashiers there is only faux frontier. It's Hilton Head come to the mountains. Range Rovers gas up at the Exxon, and several outfitter shops, closed for the season, display last year's outdoor fashion fleeces in the windows. On the higher ridges above me (approaching five thousand feet) vacation homes trouble the mountain hardwoods and outcroppings of granite. In five minutes I've traveled from Wild and Scenic to rich and famous. My only relief from a bad case of affluence anxiety is that Buzz has given me directions to a small restaurant whose parking lot I find thick with muddy pickups, the vehicles of choice of the local contractors crafting more houses on the hillsides for $250 a square foot while many of the summer people are away.

Buzz and I sit down for breakfast, starting with coffee to warm up a little. Practical and observant, Buzz notes the snow on the highest ridge tops. The snow gets him talking about water. And what, I ask, does Buzz expect from those government officials who manage the river upstream from where it disappears into Lake Tugaloo?

"I'll feel like they've done their job when a ranger can go to the bottom of the Chattooga watershed with a crystal glass and take a deep drink and feel safe," Buzz says.

Buzz is a big guy dressed comfortably in Polartec and old jeans. He wears steel-rim glasses and has a mustache that sweeps around the corners of his mouth. He's a straight-talker and drives a 4x4 pickup, a big rig that looks like something a logger would need. As we talk he pours syrup on his toast, doubles the bread over, and angles it so that the syrup doesn't drain down his arm. He has a reputation in Chattooga country for asking hard questions and demanding answers concerning management—no, stewardship—of the river. There is little small talk, and Buzz starts my education on the headwaters by telling me about one of the conservancy's shining achievements so far, securing a Conservation Technology Support Program (CTSP) grant in 1996 to fashion a conservation plan for the entire 180,000-acre Chattooga River watershed, the only plan like it at the time in the Southern Appalachians.

It's fine to think of the Chattooga River as one tine of a pitchfork whose handle tip rests in the Atlantic Ocean two hundred miles east, but Buzz reminds me to think of the area in another way, as an ecosystem or bioregion, a way of thinking about plant and animal communities and the local geography and weather that support them.

The Chattooga is part of the Southern Appalachian ecosystem, a bioregion stretching all the way from the corner of South Carolina and Georgia to southern Virginia. The Chattooga Wild and Scenic River corridor, the Blue Ridge Parkway, and the Great Smoky Mountain National Park make up three key parts of a gathering of public lands in the region comprising some 3.7 million acres. The conservation plan developed by Chattooga Conservancy calls for "cores, corridors and restoration" of ecosystems within the watershed. The idea is to protect existing mature forest, then to "restore corridors of similar habitat to link the remnants . . . to buffer all this from intensive human activity by way of restoration areas," and finally to link "on a larger scale to other forest interior blocks in the region."

Securing the health of the Chattooga is only part of the plan. "I'd like to see an area of protected land stretching all the way from Clayton, Georgia, to the Green River in North Carolina, with underpasses below major roads for wildlife."

I look around the restaurant. Home builders are often the most vocal opponents to any sort of open-space initiatives. These mountain home builders may not go for more undeveloped corridors. The land in Jackson County, where Cashiers sits and most of these men live, is already heavily government or utility owned.

"They already think we're batty, so why not dream?" Buzz says and slops eggs around on his plate.

I excuse myself to go to the bathroom, and when I return Buzz reminds me that I have just added my small contribution to one of America's Wild and Scenic Rivers. I know Buzz is right. A small resort town like Cashiers, situated high on the crest of the Blue Ridge, has to treat its sewage and flush the outflow somewhere. On one side of the ridge, the wastewater runs into the Chattooga, and on the other side, into the Cullasaja. There are now several small treatment plants in Cashiers. If, due to continued growth, a site is chosen for an additional plant, the decision will send the treated waste toward either the Atlantic or the more distant Gulf of Mexico. Either choice has an impact on the quality of the water downstream.

If water is at the heart of understanding the Chattooga, then these questions of use are the water's arteries, moving the issues around. Removing wastewater from a community is only one of the traditional industrial uses of flowing water. Generating electricity is one of the most popular: impound a fast river like the Chattooga and release the flow on demand to turn electric turbines in a power plant. This model was the backbone of the Industrial Revolution, and today there are as many as eighty thousand dams in the United States, many of them generating electricity. "They're gonna stop the river up," Lewis Medlock states over footage of a dam being built in the very first minute of the movie *Deliverance*. "There ain't gonna be no more river."

One watershed to the east, Lake Jocassee and Lake Keowee hide the Keowee River in their depths. The dark lost sister stream to the Chattooga disappeared in the early 1970s. Prompted in the 1950s by deep southern rural poverty and a growing demand for power, the Duke Energy Company quietly bought up almost one hundred thousand acres of mountain gorges, ridges, and river bottoms along the Blue Ridge front in South Carolina and North Carolina. When construction on the dam began in the 1960s, the utility cut the timber, moved out whole communities, tore down century-old farmsteads, inundated numerous major archeological sites (including Toxaway, Sugar Town, Fort Prince George, and the Cherokee town called Keowee), and relocated summer camps.

By the 1990s most of the land fronting Lake Keowee had been privately developed, and in 1996 Duke Energy announced an interest in divesting itself of the utility lands on the high, forested ridges surrounding Lake Jocassee. Duke Energy claims it has always recognized the ecological value of the vast, wooded tract as a reserve for rare and endangered species, though some say Duke's motivation for the land deal was to raise capital for other possible utility land investments.

Duke's holdings surrounding Jocassee were huge: sixty thousand acres of land in two states, South Carolina and North Carolina. In South Carolina, where two-thirds of the tract is located, the state already held 374 acres in the Eastatoe Gorge, administered through the Heritage Trust, the entity within the South Carolina Department of Natural Resources charged with land protection. Heritage Trust's purpose is to inventory, evaluate, and protect those places considered the most outstanding representatives of the state's natural and cultural heritage. The question of who would administer the Jocassee property, if the purchase went through, became a hot topic with many interest groups such as hunters, fishing enthusiasts, recreational vehicle riders, and preservationists.

In 1996 the first transaction concerning the Duke Energy property in Jocassee transpired. This was the dedication of one thousand acres as the Laurel Fork Heritage Preserve. It was the hope of many that the whole tract would be protected under Heritage Trust.

In 1999 the big deal went through and over thirty-two thousand acres entered the protection of the state of South Carolina through a cooperative acquisition between the DNR, Duke Energy, the Richard King Mellon Foundation, and the Conservation Fund. In North Carolina a smaller tract was added to the state park system. Because of the size of the South Carolina tract, and its importance as a natural resource, the purchase held everybody in the conservation world's attention—Buzz included. Some call the Jocassee Gorges purchase the most significant conservation land deal in the Southern Appalachians since the establishment of the Great Smoky Mountains National Park.

Many environmentalists like Buzz would settle for no less than administration through the Heritage Trust program, a move that would assure low-impact environmentally sensitive management, but political realities won out. A cap on the amount of land Heritage Trust could acquire by law of one hundred thousand acres state-wide did not allow for the huge purchase to be added in its entirety to the agency's properties. At the time the deal was closed, the Heritage preserves numbered over eighty thousand acres. Jocassee would push it far over the limit. Several years after the purchase, the trust's total property cap was raised to 150,000 acres, but because of the momentum of DNR policy (control would remain with the wildlife section of DNR and not Heritage Trust) no more Jocassee land was added to Heritage Trust's landholdings.

"I am not ashamed to admit my sorrow, and at times, even shed tears with the encroachment that slowly and methodically degrades the land of Jocassee Gorges," Buzz wrote once in *Chattooga Quarterly.* "The Jocassee Gorges could be managed as a great legacy for present and future generations."

Our conversation about these ridges above Lake Jocassee makes me realize how many of the environmental battles today are rearguard actions, skirmishes over remnant landscapes. It was a great victory that Duke Energy didn't sell its mountain kingdom to the developers always searching for large tracts of "view lots" for the second-home market. The victory seems hollow and short lived, like the triumphant Native American encounter with Custer. I'm a lover of rivers and find little solace in the beauty of the drowned gorges of Jocassee and the remnant lands above them. It makes me thankful that a few miles below the restaurant where we eat breakfast the sister river of the Keowee, the Chattooga, begins its rare, protected, journey.

Buzz and his wife live near Long Creek, South Carolina, close enough to the Chattooga "to hear the river through the woods a quarter of a mile away." He's developed an intimacy with the river's many personalities few possess. He's worked as a raft guide on the nationally notorious Sections III and IV. He even toured James Dickey around on the poet's last trip to the river in the late eighties during the filming of a documentary about the poet's storied life. I ask Buzz about Dickey's relationship to the river, and he has no doubt that Dickey felt some responsibility for what happened to the Chattooga—the deaths, the commercialization. When Buzz went to Columbia to see the documentary's premiere, he recalls that Dickey whispered, "Say good-bye for me to the river," as they shook hands in the reception line afterward.

But Buzz has never been willing to say good-bye. As the use of the river has grown, Buzz crusades harder and harder to secure a healthy future for the watershed. In the early nineties he tried to work within the system, as a ranger in the Sumter National Forest prior to Chattooga Conservancy's inception. During those years with the Forest Service, Buzz patrolled the river, checking boating permits and camping violations. It would seem to many the ideal job for someone in love with the river and familiar with river people. The Forest Service's idea of forest management struck Buzz as inadequate, so he left government service. The river is in Buzz's backyard and in his Forest Service district, but he still cannot carry a crystal glass down and take a drink from the river.

Buzz has an appointment to keep later in the day, so he suggests we get out of Cashiers and drop on down into Whiteside Cove to see the river and meet some of the old-timers. As we drive back down the ridge between the Chattooga and the large recreational and hydroelectric lakes to the east, I am struck once again by the meaning of this watershed divide. It's hard to imagine these rivers to the east of the Chattooga ever running wild again. They're gone, I have to admit, buried under the still, blue, watery fingers of the lakes.

But the Chattooga is still here and we drive down into its basin—mountains, free-flowing streams, forests surrounding us—and it is breathtaking. As we switch back and forth, losing altitude in the cove, I catch glimpses of Whiteside Mountain off to the north. The worn rock faces of Whiteside, the highest cliffs in the East, have the feminine curve of old mountains, but they lack the sheer boldness of the faces of Yosemite or Wyoming's Cirque of the Towers. Yet this eastern mountain would still be a powerful presence in any landscape.

It's easy to see how the sloping cliffs the Cherokee called *Sani-*

gila'gi, "the place where they took it out," figured in their myth of Spearfinger, an ogress said to have tried to build a stone bridge from the distant Hiwassee River to Whiteside Mountain in order to move easily across the rugged Blue Ridge to do her evil. Spearfinger was an early believer in the current culture's mythology, which calls for ease and efficiency of transportation. Lightning, not environmental groups, brought down her traffic project. According to the myth, the bridge was shattered with one strike from above, leaving Whiteside's cliffs as remnants of Spearfinger's stone abutments. How strange it is to wander so little distance from the suburban sprawl of Greenville-Spartanburg and see such majesty. I make a mental note to spend time just looking up at Whiteside in the right light.

The road soon crosses into the Chattooga Wild and Scenic River corridor, really no more than a creek near the town of Grimshawes. Grimshawes brags it has the smallest post office in the world, six feet by five feet and six inches, established in 1878. The tiny log building still stands on a curve of the highway, slowly falling into the frost-burnt kudzu.

I slow to glance downstream at the Chattooga. My gaze doesn't go far. At that point, five miles from Cashiers and its numerous springs and sources, the Chattooga is a swift, narrow, laurel- and rhododendron-clogged mountain stream the width of a wagon. Around Grimshawes, literally a wide spot on this mountain byway, the land flattens out, and it's easy to imagine how valuable ten acres of level bottomland would have been in earlier centuries, when corn mattered more than a view.

In 1972, Greenville attorney and environmentalist Tommy Wyche and seven others, including his son and two daughters, pulled up to Grimshawes with plans to paddle from this bridge to Lake Tugaloo, over forty miles downstream. The group loaded supplies for the five days they thought it would take in four aluminum canoes and a small raft. The Wyche family had started canoeing in the late fifties on the French Broad near Asheville and by the late sixties were regulars on the Nantahala and the lower stretches of the Chattooga.

By the early seventies Tommy and his son, Brad, had already paddled all the lower sections—I, II, III, and IV. Back then, Tommy paddled tandem with one of his daughters in a seventeen-foot aluminum Grumman. Brad paddled solo in a fifteen-foot Grumman. The end of World War II had birthed the Grumman canoe. In 1945 the Grumman Corporation set aside building Hellcats, Bearcats, and Tigercats and began manufacturing aluminum canoes that could take a pounding and stay afloat. Because of their durability, Grummans soon replaced the heavier wood-and-canvas canoes in whitewater-canoeing circles. The stories are legion in the white-water community of witnessing Grummans wrapped around boulders by unlucky or unskilled paddlers, then pried off, straightened out, and used to paddle away in when the water levels dropped.

Early in 1945 Grumman tested their prototype aluminum canoes in the rapids on Maine's Allagash River and then set about introducing fifteen-, seventeen-, and nineteen-foot models. In the first thirty years Grumman sold three hundred thousand canoes, peaking at thirty-three thousand in 1974, two years after *Deliverance* hit the theaters and millions worldwide watched an aluminum canoe wash over a Tallulah Gorge waterfall minus the movie's heroes. The company still sells them today. The Grumman canoes Tommy Wyche put in at Grimshawes in 1972 cost less than three hundred dollars. Today's models retail for more than a thousand.

The Wyche expedition put in at Grimshawes Bridge. Their four canoes and raft were loaded with camping gear and food. "The river's only that wide up there," Brad Wyche explained to me recently, holding his hands apart to show how narrow the river could be in its upper reaches. "We were probably the first to paddle the Chattooga above Section O. It was part of Dad's quest to paddle every mile of that river."

When these explorers departed, they quickly found that, in spite of their best intentions to float the river, they could barely make a mile a day hauling all their gear. Here in the shadows of Whiteside the infant river is clogged with boulders and passes through Chattooga Cliffs, a gorge with vertical walls. The river falls hundreds of feet per mile. Brad remembers dragging the canoes and raft through the water and around waterfalls in long, difficult portages.

Five days later, they still hadn't made it to Bull Pen Bridge, three miles downstream from Grimshawes. They took out, low on supplies, and walked in the direction where they hoped to find a road. To this day, they aren't sure where exactly they took out. Brad doubts he could even find the place, but they made their way back to civilization. "That wasn't a paddling trip," Brad said, remembering the ordeal. "That was a hiking trip with canoes."

As I consider the Wyche expedition and its significance—possible first descent of the upper reaches, real-life encounter with still-wild mountain river—I feel a need to follow, but I am aware that Buzz is ahead of me with his own agenda. He knows where to start this story and I trust him.

I follow him down the curvy asphalt two-lane as it drops quickly through the ancient down-cut drainage of the Chattooga. He wants to introduce me to two old-timers: ninety-year-old Tom Picklesimer and one of Tom's cousins down the road, "seventh generation living under Whiteside. If they aren't home you'll at least know where to find them."

Seventh generation. Are these the people James Dickey was so afraid of when he came to canoe in the mountains in the early 1960s? Are they the people Lewis describes to Ed in the car as the two men approach the town of Oree in the novel *Deliverance?* Lewis calls the mountain people "clannish . . . set in their ways." He says, "They'll do what they want to do, no matter what. Every family I've ever met up here has at least one relative in the penitentiary. Some of them are in for making liquor or running it, but most of them are in for murder."

Buzz pulls up Tom Picklesimer's drive. An old pickup and a sedan sit in the garage. They look to be in good repair. "We'll see if old Tom's home," Buzz says, walking along a tiny Chattooga tributary creek running past Tom's garage.

The house is red board and batten ("board and bats," as the locals say), well weathered into the hillside. Tom's side yard offers a view of Whiteside, though the porch faces the rocky stream. Buzz knocks on the door, and old Tom, wearing glasses, a red and blue flannel shirt, and old slip-on boots, comes to the open screen.

"Do I know you?" he asks.

"I'm Buzz Williams, Tom," Buzz says, raising his voice several levels. "We met at the meeting about the sewage dumped in Norton Mill Creek, and then we met again up at the church for the Barret-Norton reunion last summer."

"Williams," Tom says. "Are you the Williams boy from down the creek?"

"No, Tom," Buzz answers, "I'm from down the river, down around Long Creek."

"Long Creek?" Tom says. "I don't know any Williams from down that way. Who's this?" he says, pointing over Buzz's shoulder at me.

"This is John Lane. He's writing a book," Buzz says, quickly adding, "Tom wrote a book too. All about his family, his travels, and his growing up here in Whiteside Cove."

"Wrote a book, did you?" Tom says.

"No, Tom, he's writing a book now. About the river. He wanted to talk to you about the old times up here in the cove."

"Say what? You gotta talk loud," Tom says, sliding out from behind the screen door. "I'm stone deaf. But have a seat anyway."

The porch shades the inside of Tom's cabin, so it's dark and cool. There are several cane-bottom chairs against the wall, like something you'd see in *Foxfire*. We grab two and sit down.

"Tom," Buzz yells, "you know at the meeting we were talking about that resort dumping sewage in the creek?"

"The crick? They still dumping their sewage in the crick?"

"We're gonna sue that resort. That's too small a creek for all that sewage."

"Gonna sue 'em? Think we got a chance of winning? Take 'em all the way to the Supreme Court?"

"Well, not yet. First we got to sue 'em in the local court."

"How much will it cost?"

"I don't know yet, but we've got a local lawyer may be willing to donate some of his services, and we're gonna raise the rest of the money." Buzz tells Tom the lawyer's name and he recognizes it. I'm struck by Tom's engagement, his interest in the local problems Buzz knows so much about. Tom Picklesimer has nothing in common with Dickey's characters. I am both relieved and a little ashamed for having even considered he might.

"It gets expensive, but he's a good lawyer. One of the best around," Tom says after considering the problem a little.

The sun is bright coming in behind Tom. He focuses on Buzz, asking more questions about the creek and the lawsuit. At one point Buzz gets him telling stories about the early settlers, his ancestors. "They just come in here and said, 'See that big mountain? [Whiteside] I'm gonna move up dare.' That mountain was like a magnet."

Tom shakes his head, still upset about development. "Houses and roads," he says. "That's what's spoiled this country. They don't want to walk and see it, they don't deserve to see it."

We leave Tom standing on his porch and drive three miles down the cove road. Buzz turns up a steep narrow gravel drive, which leads for a mile past cutover cove hardwoods and then opens out into a field of planted Christmas trees. Buzz continues on until we cross a bold creek on a slab of granite. I can see from my map that it is Norton Mill Creek, the tributary of the Chattooga that Tom and Buzz have been talking about. A large country house comes into view with Whiteside Mountain as a backdrop. The house stands alone in the field. It is a white country clapboard two-story with an added Victorian turret on one end, giving it an incongruous look.

The drive ends in front of a hedge of huge old boxwoods. We park the trucks there. Buzz gets out, says, "We'll see if Mrs. Edwards is at home. She's somebody you've got to meet. She's the leader of the opposition to this sewage being dumped in Norton Mill Creek." He points up to the south flank of Whiteside Mountain, where I can make out a bristle of expensive vacation homes. "They take their water out of the Cullasaja River on the other side of the mountain and dump the treatment plant water back into Norton Mill Creek on this side of the mountain. It's too small a creek for that much outflow. We rappelled down Whiteside with a petition to stop the dumping and people came up through the woods to meet us and sign before we could even get off the rock."

We mount the neat porch. There are dozens of old tools nailed to the walls. We knock on the front door and get no answer. "Let's try one more door," Buzz says, working our way around the broad porch to the back door. Soon as we knock, a neat gray-haired woman comes to the door. She opens it a crack, a little wary of strangers. Buzz introduces himself, "Mrs. Edwards, I'm Buzz Williams, I met you at the meeting about the creek."

"It's Lombard," she corrects, warming a little. "My husband's name is Edwards. Williams? I knew you weren't somebody I knew because you came to the door nobody uses."

She invites us in, and I listen while she and Buzz talk about the creek. She says she doesn't have much, but she'll be glad to donate something to help pay for the lawyer if the water case goes to court. Buzz mentions Tom Picklesimer wants to help as well.

"You know Tom's my second cousin," she says.

"Yes ma'am, we've been down talking to him today."

Buzz gets her talking about mines, old mica mines he's heard are up there on her land. "I don't know about the mica, but you know when I was a girl we found garnets. We even had one worked down into a ring. Plowed up an Indian soapstone bowl too, not far from the house."

"You know there's soapstone behind Burrell's place on Highway 107?" Buzz says.

"Burrell's place? Used to sell beer?"

"That's it."

"All the boys knew where Burrell's place was."

Just before we leave, Buzz and Mrs. Lombard talk about the

weather. "Was that snow on the mountain this morning? I thought it was rime maybe," Mrs. Lombard adds.

Rime's not a word heard much these days, an Old English word describing a thin layer of granular ice caused by the rapid freezing of water droplets, a glaze familiar to a woman who observes the mountain every morning. Here in Whiteside Cove an old word still grips the hillsides like wind-shaped pine. Chattooga country is still the land of old-growth people—people who have lived with this place for generations—and maybe old-growth language as well.

After we leave Mrs. Lombard's we drive our pickups past where the road turns to pavement and heads back up to Highlands where we pick up a Forest Service road. Buzz stops in front of a display about a CCC camp that was located nearby in the 1930s.

The Civilian Conservation Corps had been a steady presence in the mountains during the 1930s. Venturing out from now-vanished camps like the one Buzz is pointing out, the men and women of the CCC built many of the buildings in the nearby public lands—Oconee State Park, Stumphouse Ranger Station, Walhalla Fish Hatchery. They also worked to build roads and rebuild some of the old switchback routes into the high country, such as Highway 107, the road I drove up into Cashiers that morning.

The depression-era CCC focused on concrete public projects— roads, buildings, and erosion control on the old farms of the watershed. It is becoming clear that Buzz's organization, the Chattooga Conservancy, is interested in a much more ambitious plan. "That's one of the conservancy's success stories," Buzz says, pointing to the northeast. "Those mountains are called the Fodderstacks." He points up the mountain toward Highlands. "They were some of the most sacred landscape features of this area to the Cherokee. A developer bought the whole mountain a few years ago and was going to put in a resort community. Finally he was convinced to save the place."

The pine-forested Fodderstacks are well worth saving. Some scientists have compared Fodderstacks to Yellow Mountain, a granite dome in eastern China where pilgrims climb six thousand feet to see dwarf pines. I can see from where we're parked the Fodderstacks are two domes—Fodderstack and little Fodderstack. Scientists say the dwarf and wind-twisted trees on their summits are as much as four hundred years old, maybe the best example of dwarf pitch pine in the Southern Appalachians.

Then up the road, Buzz stops to show me the Bob Padgett Tulip Poplar, a surviving old-growth hardwood on a steep slope. In 1966 a district ranger fought to save this tree, and they named it for him and set it aside as a memorial.

We work our way a hundred yards up a steep trail to the immense tree. Three or four other huge poplars share the slope above and below the ancient tree. Nurse logs rot around it and saplings spike out from the moss, still green in March. After we walk in, Buzz points out a large chestnut log dead since midcentury. This chestnut log is a ghost from an earlier life of the forest. Long ago, before industrial logging devastated these forests in the late nineteenth century, almost one-quarter of all the woods were full of the mighty chestnuts. They once covered the ridges ringing the Chattooga watershed, sometimes five hundred years old and a hundred feet tall. Beginning in the 1920s, a blight wiped out what remained of the chestnut stands, finishing the work that logging had begun. Now all that survives are logs rotting like the one Buzz points toward in the woods off the trail.

The surviving poplars are almost as impressive as the chestnut, though. We stand at the base of the huge old poplar, and Buzz explains how a tiny pocket of old growth like this one around the Bob Padgett Tulip Poplar could be the key to restoration of a fully functioning ecosystem. "In the East the problem is restoration, not preservation," he says, caressing the side of the tree estimated to be four hundred years old with a girth of twenty feet, rising 127 feet above us.

As we walk away a large owl leaves the tree's base, and I think of the owl that hunted all night from the top of Ed Gentry's pup tent in *Deliverance*.

"All night the owl kept coming back to hunt from the top of the tent," Ed says. "I not only saw his feet when he came to us; I imagined what he was doing while he was gone, floating through the trees, seeing everything."

I'm glad we see the owl near the end of our day together. It reminds me of how often events are tied together in time, what Carl Jung called synchronicity. In the novel, Dickey's adventurer heads down the river for deliverance, for escape from the deadening suburban life that the novelist saw settling over the American middle class like a shroud in the 1960s. The first night on the river, the character saw the owl hunting from the top of the tent, and it was enough to give him hope. It offered a portal into deliverance. Deliverance, Dickey's owl tells us, is a blood sport. It is dark and dwells in places far removed from the problems of the suburbs. The owl we see reminds me more of the natural beauty of this place and how protected lands also protect a certain type of rare and endangered experience.

Walking into the patch of surviving old growth with Buzz is such a moment. So much has been lost, but we are lucky to have some remnant standing. I tell Buzz about Dickey's owl, but he responds as a naturalist, not a literary critic. "Barred owl probably."

I know there isn't much restoration going on up above us on the ridge Cashiers shares with Highlands. Up there, in the thirty years since *Deliverance*, development has crept closer to the Chattooga. Up the mountain there are second houses with the square footage of palaces; people now retire full-time to the mountain communities whose populations used to shrink by 80 percent once September rolled around. The local builders laugh at the excess of custom homes, spikes of glass, cedar, and stucco clearing the trees on the exposed ridges. The builders laugh, but they make money. The high places bristle with new construction, north, south, east, and west. Air-conditioning is now standard equipment, burning electricity generated on a utility lake drowning some river once as wild and scenic as the Chattooga.

If there is a dominant vision in these resort communities today, it is the vision of the free market, of time-shares, of return on investment, of development. What I see when I ride around the old mountain roads is not a territory where someone might ponder an owl hunting at night or hope for deliverance from his deadening twenty-first-century life. Instead I see gated communities full of the shale roofs of chalets and condominiums with satellite dishes.

"I hope this has helped you some. I think you can come back now and feel like you know a few people," Buzz says as he climbs back in the pickup, ready to head down the river to Long Creek. As he drives away I notice that up on the ridges the spring snow has melted. It's started its slow, warming descent down toward the Chattooga.

The melted snow is a good sign. The water is moving into the watershed as effortlessly as I hope to. As I follow Buzz down the mountain I think about the summer people up in Cashiers and how they are like the squares of sod trucked in and planted around the guardhouses of the gated mountain vacation communities. I think of old Tom Picklesimer and Mrs. Lombard and how they are more like the four-hundred-year-old tulip poplar. They are indigenous, have somehow kept their place over generations in the watershed of the Chattooga, and have learned how to live there. Nothing shakes their relationship with the land and the river or delivers them from their responsibilities to keep that abiding faith.

Chasing Deliverance

CLAYTON,

GEORGIA

During the making of *Deliverance*

it was hard to know, really,

just where the dream left off.

Or whose dream it was.

The Summer of Deliverance

𝒯HE BANJO BOY works down at the Clayton Huddle House. His name is Billy Redden, but I haven't heard much else about him. He remains as mysterious and obscure to me today as he was the first time I saw *Deliverance*.

Near the beginning of the movie when the two cars with canoes on top pull up to the pumps of the tumbled-down gas station, the banjo boy walks from the shadows, then sits silently on the porch swing, instrument in hand. Soon Drew, played by Ronny Cox, steps out of Lewis's Scout carrying his Martin guitar, and the soft-drink salesman is caught in a call and response of guitar and banjo notes. Before the famous five-minute-long scene of "Dueling Banjos" ends, there is one unforgettable close-up of the banjo boy's ghostly, animated face with his eyes squinted shut, his mouth open in a cavernous laugh, and his tongue folded back against his perfect teeth. His face is as clear in my memory as a Walker Evans photo.

In the novel, Drew gets the boy's name and address from the boy's father, the gas station attendant, and promises to come back to the hills and play with him some other day. We see in Dickey's scene the prophecy of all the "pickin' parlors" that opened along U.S. 441 between Atlanta and the hills in the early 1970s after America discovered mountain music. In the movie, the banjo boy has no interest in the city visitor after he's finished his song. Boorman uses the encounter to underscore the distance between the cultures of city and country people. Music is the universal language, and there is a bond when "Dueling Banjos" is played. Banjo music also stands in as a sort of metaphor for the Chattooga, a shared space not quite consciously comprehended.

The encounter between the mountain boy and the city visitors shows the intricacies of being human. My notion of eastern wilderness and wildlife corridors is somewhere far upstream, but when I remember the banjo boy and Drew playing, I know I have entered the complex, long-peopled reality of the South.

Today, I'm off on my own to look for the banjo boy and other traces of *Deliverance* I might find in Clayton, Georgia. "You should be able to talk to Billy Redden," Buzz had told me in the headwaters. "And Henry Burrell's the city manager. He was mayor back then. He'll know where to find anyone else who is left from back then."

As I cross the U.S. Highway 76 bridge from South Carolina into Georgia, the Chattooga looks cold and low. If water can appear wild, then what's visible here in the river is as wild as anything upstream coming out of the higher mountains. There are dark slabs of bedrock exposed in the riverbed, and the steady current bends and hurtles around and over them. The highway bridge I cross is structural concrete from the 1970s, but just upstream the remains of the old steel-beamed bridge span the river. The rusted bridge girders are part of some crude, original thrust into the landscape, something from before the Chattooga became federally owned and commercial.

South Carolina becomes Georgia somewhere below me, the invisible boundary serious and political, the state line following the river from here downstream to the Atlantic. In the Southeast, states stand stubbornly behind the idea of "states' rights"; they also culti-vate a pride in very different personalities: South Carolina is the mythic land of rebels and rednecks; Georgia, the country of crack-ers and hillbillies. So the stereotypes go.

The Encyclopedia of Southern Culture will tell you that in Georgia, a cracker is someone living in the state's south among piney woods and grazing livestock. Up here above the gnat line, the inhabitants have been known as hillbillies. Hillbillies are mountain folk, already well on their way to stereotype by the mid-nineteenth century, though the term probably has its origins much earlier.

The amber tint of the water below reminds me of good moon-shine. Rabun County, which I've just entered, did its share to hype the hillbilly stereotype: for decades most of the illegal whiskey smuggled into Atlanta came from Rabun's hills, as did the movie *Deliverance.*

Many who glance down at the river passing below think it's pretty calm. The view from the road does not tell them it gets wilder quickly in both directions. Section III of the Chattooga officially ends just upstream of Highway 76 at Bull Sluice, one of the most famous and dangerous rapids in the world; and downstream, just out of sight, Screaming Left Turn is the first major rapid on Section IV. High-way 76 has often been the rallying point for ambulances, rescue squads, even once or twice the National Guard, all hunting the river in both directions for the casualties of its wildness.

It's still early March, too cold for paddling today, so I speed on. My truck pulls the long hill on the Georgia side of the river and passes the Forest Service's wooden sign marking the river corridor's boundary. In a few miles the road parallels the Chattooga's most impacted tributary, Stekoa Creek, which drains much of the city of Clayton, Georgia. Soon the forest falls away and the narrow flood-plain is pocked with single- and doublewide trailers with big pick-ups cooling on their huge tires out front. If there are houses, they're mostly the cheap prefab variety. A dog slinks out of a junky yard along the highway's shoulder and then bolts behind me, playing roulette with the traffic from the other direction. I pass a cinder-block fire station, punctuating my sense that things are more settled here.

When I walked around the headwaters with Buzz, I left behind the Chattooga's Wild and Scenic for the mountain front's rich and famous; the scenery of Rabun County along Stekoa Creek offers a great deal of poor and discarded. As I push up Highway 76, I'm filled with class anxiety of which I'm not proud. I came from the lower end of the socioeconomic ladder and so try not to judge the aesthetics of these houses and yards. But sometimes I can't help it. The line between poverty and wealth remains no matter how many friendly deer hunters I meet, no matter how often I stop in a country store for a hot sausage and a nostalgic Cheerwine, a soft drink as local and endangered as any warbler moving through the watershed.

Maybe it's another old, deep separation I'm feeling, that distance city people feel from the country, suburban from rural. Dickey picks up on the separation near the end of *Deliverance* in the scene where Bobby and Ed share a meal with locals at the boardinghouse. "Where do you eat Sunday lunch around here?" I once heard a tourist in a motor home ask a local woman working midday at a vegetable stand. "Home," the woman said matter-of-factly.

I felt no line as I drove around the headwaters with Buzz, surrounded by thousands of acres of government land sprinkled with only a few private inholdings. The land we explored met the criteria I had set up for Chattooga country: wild and scenic. The people we visited seemed like-minded. As I pass trailers and abandoned cars I realize that *wild* and *scenic* are words rich people might use to describe poor people. I know the "local" characters in the movie *Deliverance* were described thirty years ago in the popular press reviews as "bestial" and "primitive." *Time* described Dickey and Boorman's mountain men as "inbred to the point of idiocy," and the reviewer claimed the locals watched the city men "like weasels guarding a burrow."

Dickey knew there is a fundamental difference between the inside and the outside, the local and the distant, so he played upon it to give his river story tension. He also knew that both places—no matter how deeply out of Atlanta one ventures—are real.

Today, the local and the distant just aren't that different. As I approach Clayton on Highway 76, I leave the doublewides behind. I could be back in the resort areas around Cashiers: Kingwood Country Club appears on my right with its condos sprawling up the hillsides, its pretentious stone gates, and two golf courses. It's where the *Deliverance* stars stayed in 1971, though between then and now, it's gone through one bankruptcy and several changes of ownership. As I pass the country club I see a series of black sediment fences from construction of yet more condominiums and further expansion of the golf courses.

Buzz had told me to look for the "improvements" at the country club. Buzz claims the new developer has cleared large portions of the property, and construction has encroached on the one-hundred-foot stream buffer that exists along Stekoa Creek, the Chattooga tributary feeling the most pressure from development. It's strange how many of the Chattooga's problems started with the filming of *Deliverance,* and now, thirty years later, the issues are focused here again.

Highway 76 T-bones into Highway 441 just outside Clayton, the county seat of Rabun County, though the town is not the end of the line. For thousands of years it's been a jumping-off point for the higher mountains beyond, an old town by mountain standards incorporated in 1823 along what was then two Native American trails leading south and east. We like to think that the four-lane highways were the first efficient interstate commerce carriers, but there is archeological evidence in Ohio that huge sheets of mica were carried north out of these mountains, traded by Native American merchants on trails thousands of years ago. By 1700, deerskins and beaver skins were moving down the river to Charleston. Much of the deer trade passed near Clayton, just as most tractor trailers servicing the inner mountains pass today on U.S. 441.

One old trading trail came into town from the east by way of Warwoman Creek and Warwoman Dell. An old Cherokee myth says that a conjure woman used to wander out of the Chattooga hills once a year and make her predictions in the dell as to how the tribe would fair that year in battle.

Two centuries later invading British armies took the route into Cherokee Country in 1761 and again in 1790. In 1775, American botanist William Bartram received his first taste of southern mountains near here. After collecting plants along the Chattooga, the botanist continued on into the watershed of the Little Tennessee. Bartram's trip would later be included in his famous *Travels*.

The entrance corridor to modern Clayton is the dream not of a romantic traveler like Bartram but of a random sprawl master: a myriad of stoplights, white lines, and cars. Where Highway 76 merges with U.S. 441 I enter "the strip," where fast food reigns supreme. Every modern town has a strip. I know I can't expect the twentieth century to have bypassed Clayton. The commerce of fast food and convenience is a reality now as surely as William Bartram had an old-growth forest to project his eighteenth-century dreams on.

Clayton's city hall is a small, modern building at a four-way stop on a back street. Inside, there is a receptionist behind a counter, a woman who monitors a shortwave and answers questions for pilgrims like me. "Henry Burrell?" I ask, and she directs me through an empty courtroom, carpeted, with the multiuse look of a suburban church hall.

"I don't know much about that movie," Henry Burrell says when I ask about *Deliverance*. "I kinda wish we could forget it." He says he'd give me the names of some boys who were in it. "Maybe they'll know something," Henry says.

Mr. Burrell's in his mid-sixties, has an uplift of black hair with no gray and a strong flat face with few wrinkles. He leans back in his old office chair. It squeaks a tune as he lists those who are left in town from the movie. "Let's see, Frank Rickman's in his eighties.

He lives over across from the bank. Randall Deal is working as a dispatcher at the jail. Kenny Keener is a meter reader, but nobody can ever remember exactly what he did in the movie. And then there's Billy down at the Huddle House."

While *Deliverance* was being filmed, Henry Burrell was working as a traveling salesman. He doesn't remember much of the day-to-day. He says the town has changed a great deal since the seventies. "There wasn't much down on the strip then," he says and smiles. "Just that Dairy Queen, a KFC, and a car wash."

The chair squeaks in quicker time when Mr. Burrell begins to talk about the river, a place he obviously loves. He says he's fished it and hunted on it since he was a boy. His son Kyle finished a master's degree in wildlife at Clemson and did his thesis work on the river. "He put eighteen transmitters in eighteen trout and followed them for a year and half." Mr. Burrell says his boy still likes to fish back up in the headwaters. "He knows that river up there about as good as anybody. You ought to let him take you up there."

When I ask some history questions, Henry Burrell opens up a book and stands up. He uses my question as a chance to give me something to carry away, three pages of town history that have recently been included in an application for a new sewer plant. "We're trying to keep that plant off Stekoa Creek right out there," he says with some exasperation. "You know it drains right into the river."

I follow him into the front office, and the city manager introduces me to a meter reader. The woman has on a purple cap, purple scarf, and has long purple fingernails. It's nearly 4 P.M., and she is off duty, resting in the office for a few minutes before going home. "He's writing a book about the river and about that movie, *Deliverance*," Mr. Burrell says, working the photocopy machine.

"A book about *Deliverance*?" the meter reader says. "Well, if you see Burt Reynolds, you tell him he can kiss my ass."

Everybody laughs and a swirl of talk about the movie begins. Even the city manager takes part. "We'd like to leave *Deliverance* out of your book," Mr. Burrell says, putting the photocopied pages in order.

"That arrogant asshole bought him a place up at Sky Valley right after that," the meter reader says.

"I believe Burt's place was on King's Mountain, not up at Sky Valley," Mr. Burrell corrects.

"Henry, didn't you go down to the premiere in Atlanta?" asks the receptionist sitting behind the counter.

"Some guy came up here handing out tickets, so a bunch of us went down," Mr. Burrell says, remembering back thirty years.

"How'd you feel, seeing it on the screen?" I ask.

"Had I sat down and it been about some other place I might have liked it," the city manager says, getting serious. "But not being about here."

Three or four men and women slip in and out the front door. "The dead come alive around 4 P.M.," Mr. Burrell says, laughing as another city worker leaves and one more follows him in.

"If you want to write a book, write one about *The Great Locomotive Chase*," adds one man who has just walked in, now leaning on the counter. "Fess Parker, Jeffery Hunter, Slim Pickens," he says. "Now that was a movie. What year was that, Henry?"

"Fifty-five, fifty-six, fifty-seven?"

"Walt Disney even came to town for that one," the man remembers. "Now that's a hell of a lot better than Burt Reynolds."

"We've had lots of movies done here, not just *Deliverance*," the city manager says. "You should write about them. There's *Grizzly* with Christopher George."

"Didn't they build some big thing up at Sky Valley and burnt it down for that one?"

"That was *Grizzly*. That's the one when Two Trees, Chief Two Trees, was up there. You know, they say he was a psychic," says the man at the counter.

"When they filmed *Grizzly* they turned a car over right out there in the street," Mr. Burrell says. "It didn't go where they thought it would go. They had to do it twice."

Another city worker wanders in. "I worked on that one," the new man says, "and it wasn't *Grizzly*. It was that other one, that those two Carradine brothers were in. I worked eleven weeks on that one making the Clayton depot look like the Franklin depot. They gave me a dollar to use my voice."

"We've had movies all over here," the meter reader says. "You could write a book just about them."

"You got to talk to Billy Redden," the man at the counter adds. "You know he works right down there at the Huddle House."

I tell them that I plan to talk to him. I'm glad to get it confirmed.

"Oh yeah, he works right down the street."

"*Deliverance* was where Billy was doing that Earl Scruggs," the city manager says.

"It wasn't Billy doing the picking, Henry," the man at the counter adds. "That was Wallace Crow had his arms around him."

"Was it Wallace or Wallace Jr. doing the picking?"

"It was him, Wallace Crow."

They are all eager to get home, so I ask the city manager once again how to get to Frank Rickman's house.

"You just go on across the highway and his is that first house on the right," Mr. Burrell explains. "It's the one with the tree upside down in the yard."

"If you see Burt, you be sure to tell him he doesn't ever have to come back," the meter reader says as I close the door to Clayton's city hall.

In May of 1971 Hollywood moved like an invading army into the remote mountain town of Clayton. During six months of shooting, Hollywood used the Chattooga to create a place of natural beauty, backwoods violence, and degeneration. I'd be the first to admit that what emerged from the cutting room was not a place many would want to live, or visit, without armed guards.

We all know that the place that emerges from both Dickey's novel and the film was a work of fiction, where the characters were created for drama's sake. It was not a literal depiction of any reality, the hills around Clayton or elsewhere. Why exaggerate? Flannery O'Connor was asked the same thing. "For the near blind you have to write real big."

When I leave city hall, I have to admit I had come to Clayton looking for Dickey's larger-than-life characters and I hadn't found them at my first stop. I know Dickey liked to say that he made no distinction between fact and fiction, but I'm aware other people do. As I descend from Clayton's business district back toward 441, I reflect on my encounter with Clayton's city manager and some of its employees. The people I met were quite normal. They worked steady jobs. They dressed in comfortable, functional clothes. I recorded their conversation in my notebook, their free-flowing comments concerning Hollywood's use of their town through the ages. They expressed both pride and amusement. I admire their humor and community memory, but I did hear in the jokes about Burt and deflection of questions about the filming of *Deliverance* a sense of how deeply wounded the community had been by the film as well. They'd like *Deliverance* to go away, but I know that is impossible. This particular day's evidence is a writer appearing in their town to track *Deliverance* down. The film and its characters are as much a part of Clayton now as the Blarney stone is to that particular Irish tourist village.

I also realize as I drive away that I have something else in common with James Dickey. I don't like much of what's happened in the modern world. It is the acceptance of the modern world—like Clayton's fast-food alley and four-lane highway—that I least admire in all communities. Dickey sent Lewis and his buddies up into the hills to experience a place not sullied by what was, in the early sixties, the ubiquitous reality we all now live in—the sprawl.

Clayton stretches across the hills around me, another mainstream middle-class town, another spot where there are rich and poor in small clutches at either end of the socioeconomic scale, but most huddle in the middle. Dickey was no John Updike. He wasn't much interested as an artist in examining the problems of the middle class, outside of how to escape from them. There's no escape from the mainstream if you stay to the main highways like U.S. 441. Clayton has learned that lesson like everyone else. "The world is too much with us," Wordsworth wrote, and the world came to Clayton not long after it came to James Dickey's Atlanta.

In the early seventies, James Dickey came with his own romantic set of expectations about the mountains of north Georgia. When shooting was scheduled to start, Dickey drove his Toyota Land Cruiser up from Columbia, South Carolina, where he was the poet in residence at the university. Christopher Dickey, the poet's son, was along, his wife and young family in tow. In his memoir, *Summer of Deliverance,* the younger Dickey recalls how his father carried the trappings of his personal myth with him: guitars, bows, arrows.

"We were headed into the mountains of *Deliverance* thinking we were pioneers, but thinking, too, that we already knew our way around," the younger Dickey explains in the memoir. "This was coon-on-a-log and corn-liquor country. Grandpapa's stomping grounds. Wha-cha-know Joe's neck of the woods. 'The country of the nine-fingered people,' as it says in *Deliverance,* because there's so much inbreeding and so many bad accidents that everybody's missing something. This was a place we knew about, and knew enough to fear—but it was ours. The British director, these Hollywood crews, they wouldn't have much of a feel for north Georgia. But we Dickeys were ready for the backwoods boarding house where the toilet would be down the hall, if we were lucky, and the screen doors wouldn't quite keep out the mosquitoes."

In Clayton, the Dickeys did not get their "frontier" experience. Instead of a boarding house, they moved into "A-frame chalets around the golf course of the Kingwood Country Club." Much to the young Dickey's surprise, by 1971 Clayton was a "burgeoning resort area, an outpost of Atlanta." Hollywood would be very comfortable here.

I cross Highway 441 again and drive down Rickman Street. After the movie *Deliverance* appeared, the area may have been known as "the land of the nine-fingered people," but today the local chamber of commerce calls Clayton the place "where the spring spends the summer." In front of me on the flanks of Screamer Mountain, the hardwoods have not quite leafed out, and the roofs of vacation houses are still visible through the trees.

On my right a huge upside-down silver tree trunk with four extended limbs looms, guarding a small scrap of yard. It looks like a thick wooden tent frame. What I take to be Frank Rickman's house—squat, square, and beige—is right behind it. The place looks more like a junk store, and I nearly continue on down the road in spite of the inverted tree. I think again of Bobby's line from *Deliverance*—"This is where everything finishes up"—and wonder if the old gas station in the movie's version of Oree, with its yard full of junk cars, chains, stoves, buckets, was modeled by Boorman on Frank's yard; or whether Frank, on being told to create a mountain yard, had modeled it on his own psyche's idea of space. There is an old wrecker in the side yard like the one the Griner brothers drove in the movie. Three or four other trucks and cars sit side by side with the wrecker. Some look like they could start right now, some like their next step is the classic cinder-block perch.

A Great Dane meets me as I exit the truck. The friendly, giant dog is brindle brown and has a thick collar with silver studs. On the porch of Rickman's house are a half-dozen black saddles studded like the dog's collar and monogrammed "FR." I wonder for a surreal moment if Frank rides the big dog in Clayton parades. It follows me like a puppy as I look for the front door among the pickle buckets, chairs carved by chain saws, old tires, apple boxes. When I knock, Frank's wife answers. She's a small woman in a print summer dress and an old brown sweater. She smiles and says, "Frank's inside. Go on in." It's as if she's used to a steady stream of visitors passing back and forth through the house, hunting down Frank Rickman.

The house's interior is just like the porch. My eyes creep around the room before I see Frank sitting behind the door I've just entered. Crammed in the far corner of the room, incongruously among the flotsam of domestic life, are a grandfather clock and, beside it, a full-length oil painting of a man who looks like a cowboy. The man in the painting is huge, strong and solid, and stands holding a coiled rope. The portrait looks as if an accomplished artist has painted it. It must have cost a fortune. The portrait is so out of place that I think of the Cherokee chief Attakullaculla, one of William Bartram's contemporaries.

As a young man in 1732, Attakullaculla was one of the Cherokee leaders to meet with Sir Alexander Cuming at the townhouse on top of the Nikwasi Mound thirty miles west on the site of present-day Franklin, North Carolina. Sir Alexander convinced the young chief and five others to walk out of the Cherokee Mountains and head down the trail that now passes in front of Frank's house on the way down to Charleston to sail for London. While in England Atta-kullaculla sat for a full-length portrait in all his savage finery.

When I turn to face Frank I realize the portrait is of him. I can see the younger man in the eighty-year-old one sitting before me in a recliner. Frank has white hair and a thick ledge of mustache tilting over his upper lip. His broad hands rest in his lap like sledgeham-mers. I introduce myself and say I'm writing a book about the river, exploring how *Deliverance* has impacted the community. He smiles, stays seated, but shakes my hand, his grip still full and wrenching. "It had a hell of an impact on me," Frank says, his words sounding like they tumbled over stones in his mouth. "I was the one who added all that ugly stuff to it."

"Georgia was number three in the movie business, behind California and New York," Frank says with pride. He says he became locally famous for working with "the California people" when they came in to make movies. He built sets, scouted locations, and even did a little acting in every movie shot in the area. "I been fooling with the movie industry since *The Great Locomotive Chase*," he says, laughing. Since the 1950s he's worked on *Deliverance, The Long Riders,* and *Whiskey Mountain.* For a while Clayton was one of the primary stops on Hollywood's dream express. "It always done a right smart good around here," Frank says.

I ask Frank why so many people in town dislike Burt, and Mrs. Rickman snaps back, "Burt was always reclusive. He hid away. Jon Voight walked up and down the streets, but not Burt." Mrs. Rickman peels an orange and offers me a slice, which I take. "Burt always came by to see Frank. Frank was Burt's hero. Frank could do everything, and all Burt was was a plain ol' man."

Mrs. Rickman pulls out an old thick gray photo album, now falling apart. It's filled with pictures of Burt Reynolds and all the other stars from four decades of moviemaking. There's one fading Polaroid of a young, bearded Burt and Sally Field sitting on the same couch where Mrs. Rickman sits peeling the orange.

But Burt Reynolds is a movie star, I say. What does she mean Burt is a "plain ol' man"?

"You know, Burt couldn't hunt and ride and build the way Frank is known for."

"Burt checks on me when he's around. I got him that house up on Scaly Mountain," Frank says. "I believe Loni Anderson got it in the divorce."

"What about *Deliverance*?" I ask. "What did the locals think of it?"

"John Boorman asked me what us mountain people thought the least of, and I said a pig, but they didn't like that squealing like a pig when it showed up," Frank says, claiming to be the source of much of what's remembered about the famous rape scene. "I'd been a hog and bear hunter, that's where that pig squeaking came from."

"Are they still mad at you?"

"That's all worked off now," Frank says, smiling.

As we talk I realize that in his prime Frank was the vinyl-siding salesman of mountain culture. He cleaned up the messiness of reality. He found the places that would fit the movies and the people that looked the parts. For years he took the local and helped Hollywood make it look the way it wanted, the way popular culture wanted it to look.

"I got all the mountain people for *Deliverance*," Frank says. He found "that squinch-eyed boy" Billy Redden. "Billy's mama was raised on the old Rickman farm up in the valley. I knew he looked the part. All the California people said I couldn't show him to Boorman, but I did anyway."

Frank laughs when I ask him if Billy Redden was really playing "Dueling Banjos." Frank says Billy wasn't even holding the banjo. It was another local boy who was striking strings with his right hand and moving left hand fingers along the fret board as the banjo boy and Drew played together on the porch of the backcountry gas station. Frank says the local boy hid behind Billy and slipped his arms through a trick shirt to make it look like the banjo boy was playing. Director John Boorman dubbed in some big-time bluegrass players—Eric Weissberg and Steve Mandel—after the movie was shot.

Soon after the movie was released everybody found out the song wasn't even "Dueling Banjos," a traditional song arranged for the movie. It was a sure-enough royalty-drawing song written years earlier called "Feuding Banjos." In the 1950s, locals could have heard it on the radio in Georgia and South Carolina, played by Don Reno himself, one of its cowriters. The lawsuit that erupted after the movie came out as to who owned the song made John Boorman wish he'd headed down the river with Lewis. The issue isn't completely settled. Don Reno and Arthur Smith are still arguing about who wrote the song, even though Don Reno's dead.

Frank says that porch the banjo boy sat on wasn't really a filling station either. It was the porch on old Mrs. Andy Webb's cabin, just outside of Clayton. Frank and his crew built a road, created a gas station island, filled the Webb yard with junk, and called it a set.

Billy Redden had one more scene. Later in the movie he stands on a swinging bridge, dangling his banjo like a clock's pendulum, as Lewis, Ed, Drew, and Bobby pass below in canoes. The look on the banjo boy's face is benign indifference. Below the dangling banjo, his pickin' partner Drew floats off to the slaughter. The sound of the slowed-down refrain tells us what's downstream. Some might read that look on the banjo boy, Billy Redden, as a kind of hillbilly bliss.

Frank explains how he and another man had cut a fifty-foot hemlock "right down the middle" with a chain saw and laid the pieces end to end to make that bridge. "It took a whole day to haul it down there," Frank says, remembering his movie work fondly. "We didn't have nothing to work with but a skidder and a come-along."

Some with a weakness for mythic journeys see the banjo boy as the gatekeeper. He's guarding the border between where the hero has been and where he's headed. The old gas station and the musical duel are the *Star Wars* bar for the departing adventurers, and Ed Gentry is Luke Skywalker, the reluctant savior. The place where they make their deal is, as Bobby says, "the end of the line. . . . Where everything ends up." The wrecked cars, the collapsing shacks, and the broken glass suggest the trials ahead for the four suburbanites in their canoes. Two days later, when they come off the river, they will be wrecked. The banjo boy's dueling tune is the song that lingers over the tragedy.

These scenes were the basis of Billy Redden's fame. These movie moments are now thirty years in the past, but in the endless present of video and DVD they still flash past millions every year. People remember the banjo boy. I'd guess his recall is high among the thousands who rent *Deliverance* and the millions who tune in *Deliverance* three or four times a year when Ted Turner runs the movie on TBS.

Among *Deliverance* initiates like me the banjo boy is an icon. He's what we remember most among the movie's five or six unforgettable images. He's as memorable as Ed hunting deer in the fog, Bobby's rape, Burt Reynolds in his sleeveless wet suit, even James Dickey as the fat sheriff. "I learned to play the banjo because of that boy," a friend said to me once. "Me and five million others."

When I finally enter the Huddle House I see a man I'm sure is Billy behind the counter. He is the dishwasher, stacking just-cleaned soup bowls at a waitress station. He's skinny the way I remember the banjo boy. He wears wire-rimmed glasses to cover what Frank Rickman calls his "squench eyes," and I can see some of his teeth are gone. There's only one thing that throws me off: this dishwasher is light-skinned and ruddy, not the albino I'd expected. Either Billy has a tan or his coloring was another of Hollywood's tricks of makeup. When he looks up from the bowls I see the shape of his face, remember the banjo boy turning away when Drew offers his hand.

Billy Redden takes my hand, which I offer as I introduce myself. His hand is small. It's warm and wet from the dishwashing machine. He says he's at the end of his shift and will be glad to talk to me for a few minutes. He has another job, down Highway 441 at a barbecue house called Oinkers.

"Oinkers?" I say in disbelief.

"You know, like the pig," Billy says, smiling with embarrassment.

He has a little mopping to do before his 6 A.M. to 2 P.M. shift ends, and so I sit, drink a cup of coffee. It's already after two, and I hear Billy ask one of the two waitresses on duty if she'll stack the rest of the clean glasses for him since there's somebody here to interview him. "If he came all this way on a Thursday he must not have a job," the waitress says just loud enough for me to hear. "He can wait."

In ten minutes Billy's sitting with me in one of the booths next to the window. He's put a thin nylon black-and-white sports jacket over his Huddle House uniform and covers his head with a red, no-name baseball cap. He says he was only eleven years old when *Deliverance* was shot and he's not going to help me much. "I don't really remember nothing," he says. "Boorman just come up to the Clayton Elementary School. I was in the fourth grade. They got me out of class to say they wanted me to act in a movie."

We talked about the two scenes he'd acted in, the "Dueling Banjos" scene and the one where he stands on the log bridge above the river. He says they took a couple of days to shoot that banjo scene, and yes, it was somebody else playing the banjo. How about the house? Where was it? "It was Miss Andy's house, up on Bates Creek. It's all gone now, all changed."

And the bridge scene? "Down on Warwoman Creek, I think, on the Forest Service land." I tell him Frank Rickman said it was down on the West Fork of the Chattooga.

"That could be," Billy says. "They took it down."

I ask if he ever floated the river, and he says that for a few seasons he worked as a raft guide with a company out of Atlanta. He'd go down the river with groups of tourists interested in seeing the area with one of the stars of *Deliverance*. He stopped running the rapids after the deaths on the river. "Risking your life just ain't worth it."

Had he seen the movie many times? "A few," he says. "I enjoyed it, though I don't think they should have put that rough stuff in there."

How about Burt Reynolds? Does he ever hear from Burt or other members of the cast? "Burt didn't talk much," he says, shaking his head, "but Ronny Cox was one of the nicest guys I've ever met."

"Did they pay you well?"

"Five hundred dollars," he says.

"What did you spend it on?"

He shakes his head. "Mama got it I guess."

He turns and looks out the window toward Screamer Mountain. The banjo boy's second job is pressing down on him. I get the clue and close my notebook. Billy looks up, relieved to be rid of this ancient talk of *Deliverance*. He says, "I get a small check every six months or so, twenty dollars. Not really enough to fool with. It's been a good while since I got one. If I was them, I wouldn't even bother sending it."

Then Billy stands up, says he's sorry he can't remember much more. I say that's okay, glance down at a sparse three or four pages of notes. We shake hands again. His hands have dried. He smiles in spite of his bad teeth.

It's been thirty years since the movie crew left town. Despite Billy's brief flare of fame his life is just as much on the edge as the afflicted boy he played in *Deliverance*. If Frank Rickman is Clayton's siding salesman, its Hollywood image broker, then Billy Redden is the siding itself.

I'm disappointed as I leave Clayton. I'd hoped Billy Redden would provide the Clayton climax to my chasing the myth of *Deliverance*. Instead the mythical banjo boy in my head remains more real than the dishwasher at the Huddle House. The banjo boy is a character, one of those elements of first Dickey's, then Boorman's, myth-making. Billy Redden, the dishwasher, is the myth blurred a little too much by reality.

I knew I wouldn't get exactly what I wanted from Billy. How could I? After Drew plays so passionately, the banjo boy turns away. How could it be any different for me? I'm as much of a stranger in this country as the four men who drove up for a weekend on the river in *Deliverance*.

Soon I'll return to the Chattooga, a river I'm more comfortable with than the territory of Dickey's mythical Cahulawassee. Spring rains often bring the water levels up, and maybe I'll get a chance to chase the run-off down the river.

The Wilderness Upstream

BURRELL'S FORD

BRIDGE

TO THE

ELLICOTT

ROCK

WILDERNESS

The theory and practice of rivers
leads where nature has always
led: toward the possibility of
transcendence, toward contact
with the sacredness of the earth
and with one's better self.

CHRISTOPHER CAMUTO

A Fly Fisherman's Blue Ridge

*I*AN MARSHALL'S wearing a black and green tie-dyed T-shirt with Henry David Thoreau's head printed on the front. He's drained a cup of coffee and is nursing a serious sugar buzz from eating three Krispy Kreme doughnuts, a confection he admits he's not encountered in Altoona, Pennsylvania. A native Canadian and environmental studies professor, Ian's in Spartanburg as a visiting scholar for a symposium on bridging the gap between the sciences and the humanities, a noble cause in the settled suburbs of university and college teaching. He's promised us two days as facilitator, and I've promised him a hike before workshops begin.

It's early on a Sunday and our better selves are not awake yet. We're driving over to the Chattooga to meet Kyle Burrell, Henry Burrell's son and an environmental scientist and fishing guide now living near Atlanta. The plan's for Kyle to take us for a hike upstream into the 9,012-acre Ellicott Rock Wilderness, a steep parcel of mountain forest and riverine corridor added to the National Wilderness System in 1975.

Neither Ian nor I are fishermen and I'm afraid it shows by our attire. First there's Ian's T-shirt, which looks like something one might buy at a Grateful Dead benefit for Walden Pond. But there are other signs we are not sportsmen that will separate us from the fishermen and fisherwomen who arrive each day at the Burrell's Ford Bridge and walk up- and downstream to angle the Chattooga's waters for trout. Scanning the cab of the truck reveals my Day-Glo yellow Nalgene water bottle and both our nylon day packs and no fishing rods or waders. Looking down in the floorboard shows we're definitely from the tribe of backpackers—deep lugged leather boots, nylon liners, and wool socks.

Hiking in the backcountry makes sense to me, at least on days when floating down a river is out of the question, but nothing's ever really caught my imagination about fishing. I can see how those who love it came to love it—mastery of the technique and knowledge of the landscape being two things that are also important in kayaking. But I've never been hooked. I have to admit that I've always liked fly-fishing gear catalogs and have even purchased several shirts designed for the activity, light, airy pastel models the color of a Belize lagoon with half sleeves that can be rolled up and buttoned in place. I can see by Ian's day pack that he too likes gear. A newer model than mine, Ian's pack has a web of elastic nylon to hold extra gear that hikers often need—field glasses, water bottles, a rain jacket.

Ian is expectant and observant as he rides through this assault of new southern sensations. His experience with this part of the South is limited to one trip a few years before when he'd flown into Atlanta and had a friend drop him off at Springer Mountain to begin research for his book, *Story Lines,* a work of narrative scholarship that includes first-person accounts of hiking on the Appalachian Trail.

"You're a character today," I tell him when I pick him up at the hotel. Ian laughs and says it's only fair, since he's treated so many friends to characterization in his book and subsequent essays.

I've chosen the Chattooga hike because it's close by and I need to explore the upper reaches of the river. Watching the odometer click off the miles on the interstate, I explain to Ian that in twenty years of visits I've never seen what is known as the Commissioner's Rock, a nineteenth-century artifact on the Chattooga of political and cultural significance and a nice destination for a day hike.

The obscure mark on a stone beside the Chattooga is the secondary evidence of a survey conducted in 1811 by Major Andrew Ellicott, a Pennsylvanian like Ian, and a veteran of the famous Mason-Dixon survey in the late eighteenth century. The results of Ellicott's survey were established on a stone—the real Ellicott Rock, now lost—with "N" for North Carolina on the north side and "G" for Georgia on the south. Two years later, in 1813, another team of surveyors journeyed up the river and established the more elaborately chiseled inscription hikers see today.

I like the idea of taking Ian into a government-certified wilderness and making our shared destination a 185-year-old inscription on a rock. It seems appropriate for two writers, one southern and one whose attention has often focused on the classic nature texts of the nineteenth century—Thoreau, Burroughs, Muir.

Even though I've driven the route to the Chattooga dozens of times—I-85, 123 to Clemson, and Highway 28 into Walhalla—I soon look up and notice I've somehow missed our exit, talking, talking, talking, and now we have to cut through the countryside to get back on route. I'm a little apologetic for this battered unloved land we call the piedmont with its tract-house developments, scabs of red clay, and convenience store concrete slabs and gas pumps at every crossroad. Ian scans the countryside and says he likes the small farms of piedmont South Carolina, which still somehow survive amid all the sprawl along I-85, but admits disappointment that we haven't seen the mountains yet.

I'm thinking I want Ian to see the South as a landscape capable of reaching for the sublime, and hope there is something on the Chattooga that will convince him. He's spent his life looking for beauty in landscape and writing about it. I know it's a tough sell. It's not that the South is ugly, but it's that whatever beauty might remain is often obscured or stained for a visitor by what many consider its most obvious human ugliness—a fondness for fundamentalism, a history of racism, and the New South's well-established and documented ethic of greed. Race has not surfaced yet with us, though I think as we drive toward the Chattooga that when Ian meets our twenty-person workshop on Monday he will note presently that it is completely white. Southern fundamentalism has already become a topic of discussion between us, though. Last night Ian says he channel surfed into the presence of a local hellfire preacher, and he admits some of his clichés about the Deep South were fully engaged.

Does Ian carry into this hike a serious case of the *Deliverance* syndrome? He says he's familiar with the film, though I'm not sure whether he's read the novel. "Ah, *Deliverance* country," he said, laughing, when I told him where I planned to take him hiking today. So even the literary critic must carry the cultural clichés into this haunted landscape like a backpack.

We arrive at the Burrell's Ford turnoff on Highway 107 a little early to meet Kyle Burrell, so I keep climbing up toward the headwaters. I want to show Ian a view of Whiteside Mountain, but the road hugs the Keowee side of the ascending ridge and opens up on that watershed, not the Chattooga's. Somewhere up above us the cliffs of Whiteside are catching early sun, but Ian will have to wait until another trip to see them.

We pull in at an overlook off Highway 107 and step out of the truck. Lake Jocassee grabs my attention, impressively splayed out on the eastern horizon below us, a huge blue jewel shining among the last of the Blue Ridge before the mountains peter out in the rolling, hilly South Carolina piedmont. I wonder as I exit the truck whether this is the overlook where William Bartram paused on his journey up and over these mountains in the spring of 1771 and gazed back at the valley of the Keowee spread out below him—a "fertile vale"—he called it, and saw what looked to his eyes to be water glistening in the distance. There's no mistaking the very real lake today. From this altitude Jocassee looks like an eastern Crater Lake, I think. This is the high-country postcard view I want to show Ian to begin our journey into the real Chattooga country, a scrap of beauty to place my South up there on the sublime scale for my northern ecocritical visitor. Surely seeing Jocassee will allay any half-serious *Deliverance* fears.

It isn't until we adjust our view that we both notice a horse standing right in the middle of the overlook swishing its tail as it grazes on high spring grasses. Ian asks if it's a wild horse. I don't answer. I can't quite process the moment, and so I don't know quite what to say. My mountain script has been preempted. My tour guide spiel has been silenced by this mammal anomaly. I am prepared for deer, or black bear, hawk, or bobcat, but not for horse.

The chestnut mare is so out of place I do a 360 around the overlook and see what else might be out of place. To our left, two bikers straddle their pastel bikes known locally as crotch rockets. They mount and roar off, "Wringing the handlebar for speed / Wild to be wreckage forever," as Dickey wrote in his poem "Cherrylog Road." Then I twist even further and notice a man standing next to a little cart in the shadows, holding an old tin coffee cup.

And then I see there are two horses, the one crowding the view and another darker one tethered in the shade just off the pull-off. Both horses are beautiful and strong, well cared for. They graze and swish their tails to keep the insects moving. I am taken with this ease of motion and place. Something about it really seizes me even more than the view I had hoped would lead to the sublime.

The man next to the cart is right out of some Smoky Mountain holler or off the set for *The Grapes of Wrath,* dressed in greasy brown work pants falling down, no shirt. He's lean, right on the edge of emaciated even. His teeth are bad, and there's two days' growth of heavy black beard creeping over his face and down his neck. His hands are bony, all knuckles and axle grease.

I'm drawn to him and engage him in conversation. He is quite willing to talk, though a little cagey. I study his face and manner. He is relaxed, his fingers wrapped around the coffee cup. He says he's from over at "the foot of the Blue Ridge, Balsam Grove." He uses "you'ens" when addressing me, and his accent is so thick that I can see by the tilt of Ian's head that he is lost in this mountain man's old-growth language and accent. The man says he's come over the mountain on 281 in the little cart and is headed "over into north Georgia where they say they's good grazing for the horses and fish in the creeks." It sounds like something someone would say in 1830, soon as the soil wore out in South Carolina. He says that he cuts "laurel sticks" for a living, and I imagine him supplying those tourist shops in Cherokee with bent laurel to make chairs and fences.

I look around. The man has his minimal tools out all over the ground and an old Coleman stove set up. There's a box full of simple food—oatmeal, rice, a loaf of white bread. The little two-wheeled cart is built with salvaged boards and saplings. It rolls on two big bicycle wheels. Next to its little bench seat is a blue fifty-five-gallon drum of water for him and the horses. He tries to explain to us what has happened to the cart, something about a rope rubbing on metal until it broke, but it is impossible to follow the story, an embarrassment of communication, like negotiation deep in a rain forest with a newly contacted tribe.

I am struck by the irony of Ian's first trip into *Deliverance* country and how we've encountered this character from central casting first thing in the morning. I can see from the look on his face he doesn't know quite what to make of the scene. I think of a funny story a friend likes to tell of hiking on the Chattooga and hitching a ride in a hopped-up pickup with four guys in cowboy hats chewing Red Man. "You be careful now," they tell him as he exits the truck. "There's some rednecks around here," they warn him. "And I thought THEY were the rednecks," he laughs.

But for me there's nothing deeply scary about this man at the overlook. It's something about the horses that puts me at ease. Then I feel it. This man, though he might be slow or wounded by life and time, has that same sort of ease as the horses. I think of that phrase learned from David Abrams, "the more-than-human-world," and here it is, right in front of me, in cameo. The presence of both these horses and the man together with them on this journey adds up to more than this mountain man for me. All are wandering the mountains in the same ease.

On the long drive up from Atlanta in *Deliverance's* second section, called "September 14th," Lewis Medlock describes the country they will paddle through as a savage wilderness still only sparsely settled by humans. It's the kind of place Lewis wants to escape to when the whole world falls apart through nuclear war or anarchy. For Lewis "up here" is a place you could build something, "a kind of life that wasn't out of touch with everything."

How often I too have dreamed—like Lewis—of some such romantic escape as this in my life—Whitman's open road with no responsibilities beyond two animals to care for and a tiny cart full of basic utensils. I glance at Ian's T-shirt, and this man standing before us with his tin coffee cup strikes me for a moment as some sort of a simple Lewis or a mobile Thoreau without the Harvard education and the transcendental baggage. His cart is bigger than Lewis's *Deliverance* canoe and smaller than the cabin at Walden and surely, when adjusted for the passing centuries, cost as little or less than either. How has he done it? What has he lost in order to gain so much freedom?

I'd like to stay and ponder these questions, but the morning's appointment with Kyle Burrell pulls me back into the truck. We wish our traveler safe passage, wheel the truck back into the highway, and backtrack down 107 to the gravel Forest Service road that is the Burrell's Ford Bridge cutoff.

Kyle Burrell is taller than I expected, and younger. He's maybe thirty-five or so, slender, and dressed for comfort in the rising heat—nylon hiking shorts, a blue-checked easy-dry Columbia shirt with the tail out, and low-cut hiking shoes. He could be a high-dollar fishing guide, or dressed for work in an outfitter's store. He puts me at ease right away with his humor and pace. He listens to our story of the overlook and says we've seen someone like the Goat Man, a little man who used to wander Chattooga country in a cart pulled by four goats. "I think he's been dead for years," Kyle says, strapping his camouflage fanny pack on for our walk to Commissioner's Rock and stocking it with two water bottles. "I remember him from childhood. He was a real character. Becky, you remember the Goat Man?"

Kyle's fly-fishing buddy Becky is pulling on her chocolate-brown waders and clipping all sorts of fishing gear onto her sleeves, hat, and vest. A national champion at bone fishing, she's come over from the Atlanta area with Kyle to fish while we hike. You can tell she takes fishing very seriously, and according to Kyle, she's as good at it as it gets. "She's forgotten more about trout than most fishermen ever knew," Kyle says, nodding her way.

The Chattooga, though, is new water for Becky. She asks Kyle and he tells her about the river, what she might encounter. "There's wild browns upstream of the bridge. Downstream, there's plenty of stocked rainbows, but, as you know, fishing midday you'd have better luck if you were fishing in the middle of January. You might have some luck with the rainbows though."

Kyle hands Becky a walkie-talkie and tells her he'll call when we get back. I watch as she walks down toward the bridge across the Chattooga. I'm impressed by how much gear she's wearing. Surely the cost of all that gear must approach the cost of a kayak or the pilgrim's horses and little cart. Most of the gear I can connect to the rituals of fly-fishing, but what catches my attention and imagination is a little pair of pink flip-down glasses on the underside of the bill of her tan cap. I'm thinking it must be for the glare on the water, but then it occurs to me they are for tying tiny knots necessary for fly-fishing. Kyle's in gear to get hiking, and Becky's gone down the road before I have a chance to ask her.

Before Kyle and Becky had arrived I'd walked with Ian to the middle of the Burrell's Ford Bridge. The two fishing cultures were so obviously displayed up and downstream from the concrete span. Below the bridge there were fat men and women in lounge chairs with their spinning rods propped on forked sticks. An open can of kernel corn sat on the ground nearby. The river at Burrell's Ford Bridge is about forty- or fifty-feet wide, and its "drop and pool" character is well established. On this morning the two couples were fishing the tail end of the bridge pool and would probably take home their limit of hatchery fish—eight stocked rainbows grown to eight inches on fish meal and placed in the river—if they were lucky. Just upstream of the bridge, at the pool's beginning, in the fast water below a small ledge of dark rock, was a fly fisherman tugging his line out as the leader looped in a figure eight over his head, just like Brad Pitt in the film adapted from Norman Maclean's novella *A River Runs through It*. Even though the man was separated from the overweight couples in the lounge chairs by only one hundred yards of river he seemed in a different world. And what was so different about it? The fly fisherman was more actively engaged with the river. You could see it in his posture, his motion. It was that ease again that I had seen in the traveler at the overlook. He waded slowly down through current, casting his fly into spots on the surface that looked promising, working the line, watching the water.

When Kyle and Becky arrived I asked about the scene at the bridge and the differences I'd noted. Kyle confirmed that fishing on the Chattooga is quite a divided world—bait versus flies, spinner versus fly rod, and maybe most important, lounge chairs versus waders. There was no doubt that the bridge is the great divide. Upstream the preferred method is catch and release, though it is not required. Below Burrell's Ford, where Kyle says the Forest Service stocks forty thousand rainbow trout by helicopter once a year and thousands more off the bridge from a truck, the fishing is much more predictable and to the taste of the lounge-chair anglers. As he talked I thought of a friend's story of standing on this very bridge once and watching a truck from the hatchery throwing trout into the river and a man standing just below pulling the novice rainbows out of the current in fast order. "Why not just fish right in the tank on the truck bed?" he commented at the story's end.

"No, it's not the Goat Man," I say, walking toward the trail head, long-legged Kyle walking out in front. "This mountain man had horses. Two beautiful horses and no goats."

"Up at the 107 overlook?" Kyle says, nodding, stuffing some crackers into his pack, not surprised that the goat man has found this new manifestation. "Horses, huh? You know, on a clear day you can see the buildings in downtown Greenville from there, sixty miles away?"

Quickly we're in the woods and striding down the trail into the Ellicott Rock Wilderness, following Kyle. Ian asks if he's related to the Burrells that the bridge and ford are named after. "Way back," Kyle says. "We're all related if you go back far enough," but then he explains how he grew up over in Clayton, and he says it as if Clayton is a good distance from the river and I guess it is from this stretch. We're probably thirty miles or so by road. In this rough country bounded by tall ridges, that's a good distance.

The river runs beside us, clear and wild. Up here it's a dimpled expanse shaded by hemlock and white pines except where the sun spreads and splinters. I notice how in some of those sunny spots the blue-green surface is broken by unseen cobbles. Every few hundred yards the channel deepens into runs and broad pools. Pulled by gravity the tongues of mountain water find their way downstream even in these spots where the current looks shallow enough to wade.

Only a few minutes after we've left the parking lot Kyle says, "You guys want to see Spoon Auger falls?" We head off a short steep trail, and several hundred yards later we're standing on a little ledge of rock staring at the falls. They drop about twenty feet in several ragged descents frilled with rhododendron and mountain laurel. The laurel's still in bloom, tiny pink flowers like flying saucers fallen all over the trail.

"When I worked for the Forest Service they'd send me up the side of waterfalls to trim the limbs back," Kyle says. "What kind of fool will climb a waterfall with a chain saw?"

We soon get back to the river and Kyle's striding along. As he walks he touches plants close to the trail as he passes, literally in touch with his surroundings. Often he breaks off a branch protruding into the trail. I ask him about his master's degree his father had mentioned. He went into more detail. He had completed a Master of Science thesis from Clemson University called "Seasonal Movement of Brown Trout in the Chattooga River Watershed." He explains as we walk how most of his research was done on the water we were covering. He'd radio-tracked twenty-seven adult brown trout from November 1995 to December 1996 in the Chattooga, "the southern-most cold water stream system in the United States." He'd followed them through their fall spawning season and noted how some of them had made significant runs. One trout moved over seven kilometers from its home pool upstream into a tributary stream. Kyle had noted water temperature and hypothesized that high summer temperatures may limit the brown trout's likelihood to reproduce and grow in the Chattooga.

Kyle stops at a spot where the river is close by and he says, "This is Stovepipe Hole," and explains how all the pools and holes along the river have names and an old-timer story. "It's called Stovepipe 'cause there was a trout in there big as a stovepipe." Both Ian and I seize on this story and pull our notebooks out and scrawl down some notes. As writers we especially like this cast into the dark pool of language, the naming of things. Who could not think of Norman Maclean's novella, in which the father says that under the rocks in the river are written the names? It's that Adam gesture, and here we are on the Chattooga and we've wandered into it again.

Listening to Kyle I'm beginning to get a feeling he knows this stretch of river as intimately as anyone. He knows where the fish live. He even knows some of them by sight. These wild brown trout might stay in one place their whole lives, maybe seven or eight years in the wild. "They might have one rock that's home territory at the head of a pool, and they'll just cruise the whole pool feeding," he says. He says he was walking the trail once and stopped at Stovepipe Hole and watched a twenty-inch brown trout sitting in the current out in the middle of the pool. The sun was right so he could see the fish and it couldn't see him. He squatted on his haunches and watched. "After a while walking up the Georgia side comes a spin fisherman, just working his way upriver. He's fishing about twenty-five feet in front of the trout's nose and the fish just glides back under the ledge on my side of the river. That fisherman never knew that trout was there."

Kyle keeps walking, and on up the trail he points out two or three more of his favorite places, some where he'd had trout tagged in his study almost a decade before—Norman's Pool because there was a trout in there named Norman, Yonah Shanga Pool ("It might mean 'bear shit' in Cherokee and you know, it ended up in somebody's sleeping bag or shoe"), and our favorite, when we reach it, Jaybird Hole.

Kyle says the men who've been fishing this river forever named the holes. When we asked him how he ended up fishing, Kyle told us how his father, Henry Burrell, had brought him fishing on the river early on, even before he could recall, but that wasn't fly-fishing. He told us of one man in particular, Doug Adams, his friend, mentor, and fishing buddy from over near Clayton. "Doug's the Old Man of the River," Kyle says. "But don't you call him that," Kyle said, laughing. He explained how Doug taught him to fly-fish at fourteen while Kyle was in his Scout troop.

"Jaybird Hole got its name because the old-timers say they were walking this trail once and skirted down along this beach and there was a couple swimming here 'naked as jaybirds.' I always called it that and once I was headed up here to fish and there was this naked man and woman laid out right here." He stops and we're standing on a little sand beach and Jaybird Hole is deepening before us all the way to the Georgia side. "He was laid out face up with his hands behind his head and she was turned over on her back. It didn't matter to either one of them that we were passing by."

As we continue upstream Kyle talks a little about *Deliverance.* Though he grew up in Clayton, he was too young when it was filmed to have memories of the movie crew. Most of what he knows comes from friends. He says he was raised with many of the people who played minor roles in the film. "Everybody in that movie was real except for the two queer Hillbillies," Kyle says, laughing. "They were actors." He says he had fun in college at Western Carolina telling people that the guy who played the doctor at the end of the film was really his family doctor. "Dr. Fowler," he said. "People got a kick out of that."

Soon we've made it as far upstream as the confluence of the East Fork of the Chattooga and the main branch. Kyle says the long slow stretch of the river before us is the East Fork Pool. We stand on the log bridge crossing the East Fork, a structure known as the Forty Thousand Dollar Bridge because of the sturdiness and beauty of this particular crossing. About 2.5 miles upstream on the twenty-foot-wide East Fork is the Fish Hatchery, the birthplace of most of the hatchery fish that are stocked below the bridge at Burrell's Ford. Kyle tells a story of beginning his trout research on the river. He wanted to see where the fish were so he donned a wet suit, mask, and snorkel and cruised through the shallow pools on the narrow East Fork for several hundred yards upstream. "When I got to the rocks I had to stop and stand up. Once I stood up and there was an eight-point buck standing just above me in a pool." He tells the story leaning on the rails of the bridge, pointing upstream. "It had no idea what the hell I was. I've always thought that had I not surfaced at that moment he would have stepped right on me."

After we cross the East Fork it's still over a mile to Commissioner's Rock and Kyle hasn't slowed a notch. I'm sweating, even under the forest cover. It's hot for spring in the mountains. Kyle's still striding along with the certainty of a man who knows his territory. On the other side of the bridge, the trail widens and acquires the distinct cut of an old roadbed, and Kyle tells us that his father remembers driving down in here as a boy. After all, this was somebody's land back before the wilderness, and access is key—for fishing and logging and hunting and all the other activities and benefits people often expect from rural land. Even today, the hemlocks that surround us are not giants, and it's easy to see how sixty or seventy years ago this might have been an entirely different landscape. "Cut, and cut again," is how Kyle describes the forests along the river.

Kyle's walked this trail countless times doing his research for his master's thesis, but past the East Fork he comments more than once on how he'll soon be reaching the edge of the country that he knows well. We're far enough upriver from the bridge now that it takes more than an hour to walk out. Most fishermen don't care to cart gear and waders much further upstream. There's plenty of fishing to be done on the three miles of wild trout Chattooga water down to Burrell's Ford Bridge. As we're walking along, Kyle tells a funny story of how one year when the river flooded, the waters swamped a trout pond on a feeder stream above Commissioner's Rock and washed thousands of pond-raised rainbows downstream into the Chattooga. "There were sixteen-inch rainbows all through here," Kyle said. "People came up and cleaned them out with night crawlers. It was like fishing out west for a day or two, though, of course, those fish were real dumb."

Suddenly, in the middle of the trail, Kyle stops. "Here it is," he says, pointing down toward the water at a sloping rock partially 1hidden under overhanging rhododendron and mountain laurel. "Ellicott Rock."

I look down toward the river and the spot that looks no different from any other along the preceding two miles of river. A sloping ledge. Swift current. There's an island in the river and so it's narrowed to creek width. I note a small wisp of orange flagging tape hanging on a low hemlock branch, but besides that, there's nothing else visible. A long way from sublime, I'm thinking as we follow Kyle, rhododendron to rhododendron, in his short scramble down to the water's edge. Soon he's squatting on the slanting dark rock looking down at an inscription. We huddle around. The water's so loud down next to the river it's almost hard to hear each other. "LAT 35 AD 1813 NC + SC," the chiseled inscription reads, the three bits of information stacked one on top of the other.

Walking above the river I had never really been fully aware of the water running a few feet below the trail. Now, a short scramble down, the water is, as Dickey describes it in *Deliverance*, "profound, its motion built into it by the composition of the earth for hundreds of miles upstream and down, and by thousands of years." Though the Chattooga isn't quite that long (less than one hundred miles total), I sense what Dickey documented with a perfect poet's sensibility. The Chattooga moves by with immense presence and purpose. It circulates molecule by molecule through the channel and down past us and the rock where we sit.

It's a good place to eat lunch, so we all take our boots off and find a comfortable place to sit on the mossy ledge tucked hard into the stream bank. As we sit and eat, Ian says that he's disappointed, that he wanted his picture taken standing in North Carolina, South Carolina, and Georgia all at the same time. Kyle says the middle of the stream is the Georgia line. "You have to get your ass in Georgia and your feet in North Carolina and South Carolina," Kyle jokes, pointing out to the middle of the swift cold stream.

"How would a modern-day team survey this border?" I ask Kyle, a man who does some surveying in his work. "You'd start with a known position," he says. "There's a USGS position down at the bridge. You'd start there and run transverses all the way up here."

Sitting on this rock ledge next to the Chattooga, I'm bounded on one side by this "text" from the early nineteenth century, a cold chiseled location marker to mediate a forgotten and almost impossible to imagine political dispute between two states, and on the other by the wild living river itself, owned by nobody, controlled by nothing but last night's rainfall.

The Wild and Scenic Chattooga flows and flows, unceasing, making a racket as it drops a few inches over the tiny stair-stepping ledges below us. This is the music of erosion, and over time the river will take this mark left by a team of surveyors almost two hundred years in the past. This spot will be lost as sure as the original Ellicott rock is lost somewhere in the forest or river.

This is the southern sublime, not the overlook experience I showed Ian this morning high over Lake Jocassee. Sublime in the southern wilderness is always closed in, cramped by trees, cliffs, hills. Everything closes in on you down here, everything close enough to touch, both the beautiful and the ugly. If you can't see beauty in closeness you'll really never see it in the South.

I take a bite of my cheese cracker and stare out at the moving current for a little perspective, then I turn full-face into the wet stone so near my ear. I can see and smell a trickling seepage from within the bank. A tiny world of ferns and wort form a miniature Serengeti an inch from my nose. I disappear into this tiny square foot of wilderness, and I feel what Annie Dillard described in *Pilgrim at Tinker Creek* three decades ago. Southern beauty is full of moments and surprises usually associated with nearby places closed off from the world.

I nearly say aloud what I'm feeling, but I know I need to be careful bringing the sublime up in the presence of an ecocritic. Ian understands the antecedents of *sublime* as a dissertation-trained literary critic might. He probably hears in it a term rooted in Romanticism, the idea, as Roderick Nash explains in *Wilderness and the American Mind,* that "sublimity [suggests] the association with God and wild nature."

That's not how I'm feeling here with this wild, free-flowing river just out of my reach. I'm sprawled out, my elbow resting on bedrock. This spot is wild nature, in spite of the towns in the headwaters and the highways and this pioneer surveyor's petroglyph. God is present in chemical weathering of the rock, the variety of species, if you believe, as I do, that God is the image of all natural process, including the evolution that formed my eyes and hands.

In the past, Nash says, wilderness appealed to those "bored or disgusted with man and his works." What walks us today three miles up from Burrell's Ford Bridge where some of the fishermen sit in lounge chairs and pull human-grown hatchery trout from the very waters we watch flow past this wild spot? It's some attachment crossed with independence that Kyle Burrell knows when he comes up here to fish, but is it that same attachment the Goat Man was looking for thirty years ago and the Cart Man at the Jocassee overlook is even now chasing through the mountains? "There's good grazing for the horses and fish in the streams," the Cart Man said when I asked him why he was headed into north Georgia. Is it what Lewis feels in *Deliverance* when he first glimpses the river through parted foliage, the Chevy Blazer idling behind him? I listen to the river for the answer. I turn my attention to the tiny forest of wet ferns at my ear. Kyle and Ian take off their shoes and dangle both feet in the cold current. "It'll make the swelling go down," Kyle says. "And it feels so good."

Trail Mind

RUSSELL BRIDGE

TO

LICK LOG

CREEK

Backpacking calls out the

wilderness inside ourselves,

and we're always surprised

by its sane and gentle nature.

ALBERT SAIJO

The Backpacker

*I*N MID-MARCH I approach the Chattooga Wild and Scenic River corridor from the northeast on South Carolina Highway 28. I can think of no better way of spending a weekend than backpacking in the remote country above Russell Bridge. In *Pilgrim at Tinker Creek* Annie Dillard sits under a sycamore simply to "watch new water come down the creek." I want more than that, but I'm not sure what. I know I want the next two days to offer up some silence, and some reintroduction to the Chattooga, which I haven't seen in several weeks.

I'm with Terry Ferguson, chairman of South Carolina's Heritage Trust Board, and Wofford College geologist. Terry's an old friend, a serious scientist with a softer side informed by James Joyce and depth psychology. Ours is the type of intellectual friendship that's possible at a small liberal arts college, and we cultivate it— poet and scientist—as much as possible across disciplines.

We're driving in my blue Toyota truck. My dog Ellie Mae is in the back, hanging her head out of one of the tiny windows of the camper top, catching the breeze. It's warm already, approaching seventy, and we've got the windows down in the cab as well, following Ellie's lead. She is both poet and scientist, exploiting the moment, reveling in the air, experimenting with velocity, her ears at a gaudy right angle to her head.

Ellie is a cross between a beagle and basset. Her body is too big, head too small, legs long but spindly. Though people make fun of her, Ellie has had her fifteen minutes of fame; in 1996 she was featured in a large picture in the Perception kayaks catalog, and every time we went near a river that year people would stop, stare, and say, "Hey, that's the Perception dog!"

Along Highway 28 we see yard sales, peanuts boiling in black kettles, and pigskins hanging in cellophane bags. We aren't in the backcountry yet, but not far west the blue haze of the mountains is distinct and inviting.

"I haven't had a pack on in six years," Terry moans as he shifts in his seat. "I'm out of hiking shape."

"And we're both fat," I smile.

"A sad commentary on our state of affairs."

Though now he spends more time staring at a computer monitor or chairing meetings where people talk about valuable natural places like the Chattooga, Terry's had his share of youthful outdoor excess. All the way from Spartanburg he tells stories of the deep past, of climbing the sheer rock faces that mark the country just west of us. As a college student at Wofford, Terry climbed most of the rock faces known to the native peoples as the Blue Wall. He tells of taking a long fall in one place, of another time getting stuck on Table Rock when a storm moved in and having to bivouac on the cliff face, 750 feet from the valley floor.

The last time we hiked together was 1993, in the Wind River Range of Wyoming. We packed into the Cirque of the Towers with a group from Dallas, including Terry's geologist brother, John. It was pure western wilderness country. We hiked in ten miles over two ten-thousand-foot passes carrying hundred-pound packs. John still likes to tell the story of how Terry and I stowed bananas in our packs. When we arrived at the campsite, they were mashed throughout the rest of our gear. It took an entire afternoon to clean everything—sleeping bag, tent, and clothes. "It seemed like a good idea in the grocery store," Terry laughs when I bring it up.

That was a climbing trip. Well, Terry climbed with his brother, and I sat and watched them with binoculars from my Crazy Creek chair. I don't mind climbing, but the rappelling has always sent me into shock, and all the climbs in the cirque require multiple pitches, ending in multiple rappels. I was happy to watch, to do some easy fishing for the dumb, stocked rainbows in the high lakes, to hike around the cirque and disappear off the radar for ten days. In the seven years in between, our lives had gotten busier, even though we have vowed time and again to drag the packs out, clean the camp stove of crud, avoid the bananas, and go back into the woods together.

Where we're heading is as close as you can get to wilderness within a hundred miles of Spartanburg. It's not deep country—the Chattooga corridor is only half a mile wide—but in places such as the section of trail we've chosen to hike, the Forest Service land pads the river from farming, logging, and home building.

What we drive through on the way to the river is a long way from wilderness though. South Carolina's rural counties aren't much on zoning, and even after we get out of the I-85 corridor, a three-hundred-mile superslab all the way from Atlanta to Raleigh, the rural backroads' rights-of-way are cobbled with spindly tree farms, gaudy commercial and residential development. This sprawl of asphalt and lawns is what the local county commissioners call progress, but I can't help but think of every trailer park and minimart as a stake in the heart of what was once the most extensive temperate forest on earth.

Walhalla, about fifteen miles from the Chattooga, is the jump-off point for the wilder edges of South Carolina. It is a town with a shadow of its early self, a town where fast food hasn't driven out the last mom and pop café on Main Street, where the city council hasn't voted to jerk down the Confederate memorial as if it were some statue of Joseph Stalin.

You can smell the undeveloped country from Walhalla if the wind's blowing east. Soon as we cruise through town (right down Main Street), apple stands (though boarded up in April) begin to appear on the dusty shoulders of roads. The hardwoods get thicker there and the hills begin to form on the outskirts. The highways are gnawed on the edges from weather a few degrees colder in the winter. There are more dead wild animals on the road—possums, raccoons, squirrels—than dogs.

The highway out of Walhalla (which sits at about a thousand feet above sea level) begins to curve and climb, gaining altitude. It picks up nearly a thousand feet in a hurry. The Walhalla hills quickly take on the dreamy aspects of low mountains, and we know we're right on the mountain front, which isn't as extreme here as it is in other places along the Blue Ridge escarpment. Terry explains how, here, in this remote corner of South Carolina, Georgia, and North Carolina, you actually pick up the uplift in two pieces, one here on Highway 28 and another in the Chattooga headwater country climbing into Cashiers and Highlands.

A few miles further on we begin to drive through thick stands of public forest, Sumter National Forest, interspersed with private land. There is mud on the highway where numerous red clay roads empty into Highway 28. There are big semis rolling along the highway piled high with scuffed up hardwood logs. Most of the logs are twelve to fifteen feet long, so each truck really carries two loads, one on the front of the trailer and one on the back. It's not like some rare places out west. You don't see the trucks leaving the forest with four or five logs spanning the whole forty-foot trailer.

We pass Stumphouse Tunnel Park, and Terry comments on how somebody's logged right up to the edge of the picnic area. Stumphouse Tunnel was the end of the line for an effort to push a railroad into the mountains before the Civil War. You used to be able to walk the half mile into the darkness, flip off your flashlight, and feel like you were in the growling belly of the mountains. It was one of the wildest experiences in the region. Terry says they closed it out of caution, afraid someone would be injured in the dark. I hate that the tunnel is closed, another wild and endangered experience off-limits, and I curse the excesses of caution, and mourn the dark space lost deep within the mountain.

I note that the forest we're passing has been clear-cut, an aspect of traditional forestry known as even-age management, an innocuous term for it. The more radical and fringe have other names for it. "Damn clear-cut" comes quickly to mind. I know the bottom-line rationale for this sort of cutting, but it still buries a spike in my gut when I see it. I'll try to explain in reasonable tones though for the sake of balance: In even-age management, tree removal is patterned after catastrophic natural events such as wind, fire, ice storms, and disease. Beside clear-cutting, the other even-age technique is the seed-tree cut, which removes most of the trees while leaving healthy seed-producing trees, which are also harvested after the new stand is established. There is even a science—silviculture—developed to aid in the production of timber for salable wood products. For the past one hundred years, preventing habitat destruction and protecting against the loss of biological diversity have not been near the top of the list of values for many foresters. *Maximum yield* has been the watchword of the industry.

Clear-cutting is the primary operation that has sustained the maximum yield program through the last century. Clear-cutting removes all trees larger than one inch in diameter. Certain trees are often left in a clear-cut—wildlife habitat trees, for example—but mostly a clear-cut scrapes the land clean. A clear-cut has another advantage to forest managers besides yield: it maximizes available sunlight for new growth. The downsides are many though. Usually a mixed hardwood forest, when clear-cut, is planted back in a single species of tree. A stand of oak, hemlock, and poplar becomes a stand of even-aged pines planted in rows. The battle by conservationists and preservationists against clear-cutting has been raging for years.

Logging presents a dilemma for a writer as well. I probably use enough paper in a year to clear-cut more than a few acres, but every time I see the physical results of a clear-cut logging operation—the slash piles, the skidder ruts, the stump fields—it's enough to make me pause my cursor and unplug my laser printer.

There is a new value system for forestry, and I know that Buzz Williams is a proponent of it. "There is one overriding factor that separates new forestry from traditional forestry," Buzz explains in one of the issues of the *Chattooga Quarterly*, "the decision about the ultimate values for which a forest is managed. Traditional forestry tends to approach forest management from the perspective of the monetary values to be derived from commercial species. New forestry looks at the whole system."

In the new forestry, trees are managed in uneven-age stands. They are harvested through group selection, where cutting one- and two-acre stands creates openings for regeneration of trees. The individual tree is also selected. In this method, trees of various sizes dispersed throughout a forest are cut.

In the Chattooga River watershed, where we are headed, the terrain is mountainous and there is high rainfall. The forests are multilayered, lending them best, Buzz says, to uneven-age management, but all we have to do is look around us as we drive in to see that old forestry techniques still hold their popularity.

Terry smiles his scientist smile as I start into a tirade about clear-cutting, getting louder with every curve. "I'm for big trees," I say, my grip tightening on the steering wheel. "Huge trees. Lots of them."

For a moment I realize I sound a little like Lewis early on in *Deliverance*. If Terry knew the novel well, he might be expecting me to spiral into some sort of back-to-the-land sermon against the Forest Service, the government, and the coming doom from over-regulation and civilization of all sorts. Long expanses of green are definitely part of the myth of wilderness in the east. Often, the woods still stretch for miles in the rural South. Ownership determines whether each stretch is destined to fuel a college-educated sense of big-tree sublime or keep the chip mills and laser printers operating for another week.

Is *Deliverance* an environmental text? Does Lewis have these sorts of forestry-value questions in mind when he preaches to Ed as they drive into the woods of north Georgia? Most literary critics would claim that I'm losing track of the book's heart if I spend too much time thinking about the economic impact of clear-cutting as a theme in the first section of the novel or pour over camera angles aimed at the misty mountain woods in the opening scenes of the film. They would point out that in traditional criticism character trumps setting, and certainly character would trump a theme such as the exploitation of a natural resource.

Environmental text or not, I have always loved the way the *Deliverance* character Lewis Medlock foregrounds the problem of wild country and our relationship to it. Lewis wants to move to Costa Rica to get away from Atlanta's early "sprawl" long before the word had found its vogue. Early in the novel Lewis becomes an evangelist for the wild, its deep woods and raging waters. Forty years later we're driving through the same problem on our weekend getaway to the wild.

We wind through these multilayered forests on Highway 28 as we work down toward the river, losing altitude on a series of switchbacks. The river flattens out at Russell Bridge, where Highway 28 comes in from Walhalla and crosses the river. It's here, downstream from Russell Bridge, where *Deliverance's* Chattooga begins. Down here, the drop/pool topography of Sections II, III, and IV takes hold of the river and the imagination. Upstream where we're headed everything is much more subtle. It's called Section I and it's all hiking, fly-fishing, and illegal inner-tubing.

When I look at my topo maps it seems as if the great Chattooga ridge running northeast/southwest up- and downstream has been pushed apart here at Russell Bridge, opening out for a half mile or so. Perfect river-bottom farming country of the past. As if on cue, we pass on the South Carolina side of the bridge the old Russell homestead, now a Forest Service–maintained historic site, with parking lot, tumbled-down chimney, and old barn. During the nineteenth century this old house, still standing until 1991, was a wagon stop for travelers headed the fifteen miles further on to the resort community of Highlands, North Carolina. This was the last the Charlestonians, in flight from summer heat and malaria, saw of South Carolina.

We park on the Forest Service road that serves as a trail head on the South Carolina side of the river. The road is lined with cars. A cobalt blue April Saturday brings them out. In front of my Toyota pickup is a Mazda pickup with a suburban Atlanta tag. The tailgate is down. In the bed of the truck are three petite women struggling with huge backpacks as if they are wrestling angels. A large yellow Labrador waits patiently beside the truck, doggie saddlebags already strapped on its broad back. This dog will carry its own food up the trail. My beagle-basset jumps out of the truck and eyes the trail-equipped Labrador with suspicion.

"Two or three miles in I'll wish I had equipped you with one of those," I say to the dog.

"She's a celebrity," Terry reminds me. "She's used to somebody else carrying her load."

The women manage to fit on their packs and head off up the trail, their dog taking the point. The literary irony is slurry thick as they head down the trail. In the plot of *Deliverance*, these are the women that were left behind. Now, they light out, like Huck Finn, for the territories, with some clear sense of freedom and wildness motivating them. I'm all for these developments, but I can't help but wonder what Lewis (or Dickey) would think of three Atlanta women and their dog backpacking alone in this isolated corner of the South. I watch their packs disappear up the trail.

It's midafternoon, crisp and clear. We're late getting started, but the plan is to hike four miles to Lick Log Creek and camp there, walk out the next morning, Sunday. Along the way I'm hoping Terry will explain the geology of this section of the Chattooga to me. One of his best qualities is that he tolerates the questions of novices and enlists the right analogy to make a landscape's dynamics make sense.

I'm in a blur as we begin to walk in. Nothing registers. I'm still on suburban time and looking through suburban eyes. It's as if the residue of the other world has to drain back into the rich Chattooga soil before I can really *see* anything. There are gnats already, though it is only April. I see them, hear them buzzing around my face. The trail—known along this section as the Chattooga River Trail—skirts a large section of bottomland for three or four hundred yards before hugging the shoulder of the river for two miles to Lick Log Creek. As we walk the old logging trail above the bottom, we hear many people camped in the cane and saplings of the old bottom. At one point we get a glimpse of one camp—what looks like people familiar with a particular favorite weekend campsite, comfortable in old-style canvas "house" tents, huge coolers, grills, chairs, even the back-seat of a van—hauled the short distance from the parking lot.

It's good to see these people camping on the river. Soon after the establishment of the Wild and Scenic River in 1974 many in this isolated corner of South Carolina felt they had lost their river, a place that had provided generations' worth of fishing, hunting, a place to hold picnics and church services. In the seventies there were threats to burn down the whole river corridor. For a while, in every contact between locals and outsiders, there was the potential for violence.

"They pulled it over on us," a journalist quoted one local woman as saying in the early eighties, speaking of the creation of the Wild and Scenic River corridor, "and we didn't even know what had happened until it was already done."

"They," the journalist explained, was a term used "collectively to describe the U.S. Forest Service and the tens of thousands of white water boaters who come annually to run the river." I imagined it referred to hikers like us as well.

Ted Craig, then district ranger for Andrew Pickens National Forest, explained it this way to Jim Tharpe, a news writer for the *Greenville News* in 1980. Craig said, back then, the locals wanted two things: "Open up the roads and exclude people from the outside. Some of them wanted us to start checking driver's licenses and make people from outside Oconee County leave the area. They didn't seem to realize that these are national lands, and that we have to manage them for the nation as a whole rather than any special interest group."

What is the special interest this group called locals wants from their management? It seems to be isolation. For this I can't quite blame them. I like nothing better than being left alone when I'm out hiking or boating on the Chattooga. That's my special interest in coming here. I want to be alone, or with one or two friends. If I wanted crowds I'd go to Six Flags. A whole value system rooted in isolation forms in the question "You ain't from around here, are you?"

This tension between the more communal life of the city and the isolated life of the rugged individual is at the narrative heart of *Deliverance.* We feel it when we park our car and leave the paved roads behind. We sense it rising from the encampment hidden here in the river bottom, so near to the road. We are walking away from people, hoping to find a little bit of solitude, even isolation, on this government-managed land.

In a few minutes we've settled into our packs. We've got all we need for the weekend. We're each carrying about thirty pounds. We have a tarp, but no tent. A change of clothes, sleeping bag, ground pad, stove, and pots. We have enough food for two days. I think for a moment how old man Russell must have broken his back on a generation's worth of corn in this bottom and how now it's growing a generation of fun—Hank Williams Jr., Budweiser, and fishing for the people camped below. What do they think of the backpackers passing them on the high trail? We leave that question unanswered and start a sharp, short climb to the trail beside the river.

We're between 1,700 and 1,800 feet in elevation along the river. The ridges on each side, the boundaries of the Wild and Scenic River corridor, top out at 2,300 feet. Russell Mountain, above us, is the highest point, 2,535. Not really high country, but high enough to change the weather, the vegetation. Already we are picking up hemlock, rhododendron.

I take the point, set a pace that is comfortable for me, and don't worry about Terry. My experience hiking with Terry is that he is slow the first day but quickly strengthens. He has on a blue polypro toboggan and dark blue polypro undershirt. By the second day he's usually setting the pace, no matter how long it's been since he's been in the woods.

The trail twists and turns around the ridges and we cross several small creeks and even pass a small waterfall, where the women we'd seen in the parking lot have already stopped for lunch. Soon after, Terry says he needs a "pit stop" and digs the toilet paper out of his pack. He sets his pack down and heads off up the trail for privacy. Soon after he disappears around the next bend, the pack decides to tumble forty feet into a steep creek bed. I watch in disbelief as the pack rolls over the edge, a cobalt blue tumbling mass, slinging water bottles in several directions, until it finally rests against a sapling. I decide to wait until Terry returns to do anything about it and note in my journal a wildflower I've seen blooming on the trail—the dwarf crested iris *(Iris cristata)*, dark purple flowers with three-inch vivid green V swordlike leaves coming up through the dry leaves. The field guide says they are found in rich woods, banks, and bluffs. This trail fits all three.

When Terry returns, I point out where his pack has landed. He shakes his head in disbelief and explains the geologic term *angle of repose*, how an object stays in motion until it reaches equilibrium. I listen to Terry's definition of what happened to his pack, then traverse down to retrieve it, passing it up to Terry's waiting grasp. This is one of Terry's best qualities, to turn anything into a teaching moment. I help him slip back into the recovered pack, and he departs ahead of me down the narrow trail, still explaining the physical dynamics of objects in motion. We too are in motion, I note, toward our distant campsite, our own personal angles of repose.

Most of the Chattooga watershed we pass through was logged a century ago, though even then no old-growth forest. The trees along the trail have some size, have leafed out a little already, and make the walk cool and shaded. The trail hasn't been cleared yet this year, and we twist down and under several weather-downed logs, big brittle hemlocks with limbs like porcupine quills. Sometimes, when the shoulder of the mountain is right next to the trail and the trail falls off twenty feet below, we have to remove our packs to get around, over, through the downed timber. After an hour we decide we need a water break, sit on a downed log. Two hikers come up the trail, maybe college boys. They each have twin ski poles, shorts, and gaiters. They tell us they've gone down the other side of the river—bushwhacking—and they forded the river an hour upstream, and now they are headed down to Russell Bridge. They tell us there is a great camping spot "about fifty minutes" on along, right next to a waterfall. We agree that this camping spot will be our goal. Two hours is plenty to walk this first day.

An hour later we've reached the junction of the Chattooga and Bartram Trails. Here, just below the area of the river known as Rock Gorge, the Bartram Trail heads east, away from the river, up Lick Log Creek. The topography around us begins to get steeper. The river, a little wilder.

I stop for a moment and look up and downstream. Here the river is pure mountain. There are small ledges that break the surface every twenty yards or so. Every scrap of stream bank seems to contribute to the river's flowing. There are seeps in the hemlock woods and spring burblings falling from the trailside and two or three small creeks adding a few cubic feet to the steady current.

Walking the trail up Lick Log Creek, we pass a loud waterfall, probably the one the hikers told us about, but follow the creek further away from the river to the junction of the two trails. A few hundred yards from the river we rest in the presence of another, bigger waterfall. It's a broad drop of twenty feet in two broken slides, choked with rhododendron. There is a pool at the bottom snarled with old logs washed over the falls in floodwaters and dried to a silvery sheen over years. It's the river's equivalent of driftwood. Ellie wades in up to her belly and drinks deep and long as only a dog can do, lapping for minutes at the cold water. The waterfall is not a classic wiry drop but very beautiful and wild anyway and it's easy to see why it's such a popular destination. It's an easy hike in, flat ground, and a possibility of solitude.

But this time, solitude is for another weekend. It may be wild and scenic here but it's not isolated. There are already three large loud groups camped just downstream of the waterfall. We can see their brightly colored backpacking tents through the thin spring foliage. A girl in Teva sandals says hello, wades into the pool, and dips a water bucket just below the waterfall, then carries it back down to one of the camps. We walk down and check out the possibilities for campsites, but decide to backtrack to the river and camp there. Too many people at the waterfall. "Location, location, location," we laugh and head away from the prime real estate.

It's the next morning and we're hiking out. We've broken camp, packed, cleaned up, and now are walking back toward Russell Bridge. The night was unexpectedly cold, with temperatures in the low thirties. It was so cold that Ellie tried repeatedly all night to crawl inside my sleeping bag. Terry woke up once, and he says we looked like some strange beast, Ellie's tail and hind quarters trailing out of the bag. We camped right next to the river, interrupted only once by a fisherman walking a trail right along the river's edge. Near dusk, in a surreal moment, a large group of Scouts came up the trail with huge packs and all wearing orange toboggans. They continued up toward the waterfalls and the more high-rent real estate.

We picked a good site with an old fire ring and a buffer of birches between us and the trail. A large rapid, just upstream, kept up a jumble of rock music all night.

"You need to talk about the sound—the sound of the river," Terry says as we are walking away from our campsite in full packs. I think of the way Barry Lopez has described the proper approach to an Oregon river in *River Notes:* "Kneel with your ear to the water; beyond the *plorp* of it in a hollow and the sloshing gurgle through labyrinthine gravels, are the more distant sounds of its fugue." I wonder if this is what Terry means: to find my way into the river and its sound, its texture.

We are moving much slower today, watching, listening, and smelling. Terry says the river has many voices, not just one. He says if there were time, we could sort out so much by the different sounds the river makes in different seasons. Today the river rushes over stones but it is not high, not moving things around. It is speaking in a low voice, not much above a whisper. Terry tells me how during a big spring flood, or when a fall hurricane moves through, a river this size will sound like a bowling alley, with rocks cracking against each other as they literally roll along the bottom of the river.

"All these rocks are on their way to the sea," he says, pointing out the boulders cobbling the river bottom. "You see how they are all tilted downstream, waiting for the next flood? They just roll over like snowmen." When the velocity is great enough, Terry explains, they all roll into motion. They flip over and roll. "This is the original rock and roll."

We had not noticed walking it the day before, but the trail cuts through much flatland as it swings away from the river for a mile. "Old farm fields?" I ask Terry.

Always the scientific skeptic, Terry answers "*Could* be." Could be, might be, and maybe—these are Terry's stock responses; hardly ever does he say something *is*. "Might be a log landing from the old logging days too."

I mention that a historian I know has speculated that the Chattooga remained sparsely settled because a narrow rocky valley is mostly unsuitable for agriculture. "Sparsely settled by white farming people," Terry points out. The undercut rocks and boulders made this valley fine habitat for aboriginal peoples thousands of years ago, pre-Cherokee. They camped in rock shelters, fishing and hunting. Now, in this period, the geology makes for nomads of a different sort, white-water paddlers. "Farming's a fine way to make a living, but settlement's a matter of perspective."

Then we see, just to the left of the trail, an old house site, unmistakable because of its standing chimney. "Definitely old fields," Terry smiles. "Late nineteenth or early twentieth century probably."

Twelve feet tall, the chimney looks as though it could still work if pressed into service. The old gray stones have lost the mortar that bound them together. They are cold to the touch on this early April morning.

Green tufts of daffodils are already up nearby. Small saplings of poplar and maple have grown up all around the house site where the yard used to be, and they stretch into the near distance, where some backcountry farmer planted corn within earshot of the river. I think how this is such a common moment in the corridor—an old chimney, and the yellow or white daffodils left behind to bloom each year after abandonment. Since the turn of the nineteenth century, almost 75 percent of the land in the Chattooga watershed has passed from private owners and power companies to the U.S. Forest Service.

In the woods we see a native plant that interests Terry: running cedar, or *Lycopodium complanatum*, also known as Christmas green, or trailing evergreen. It's a prolific propagator and sometimes it not only runs but leaps as well. "It's a living fossil, old as the rocks," Terry says, squatting down to pick up the strands of scaly evergreen that he says has a fossil record dating back three hundred million years. "It's like dinosaurs. They didn't die out. They are all around us, evolved into birds. And the pine tree ancestors are one hundred million years older than the hardwoods."

As if on cue, we are soon walking through a small section of planted pine, and the woods are already beginning to smell hot and piney. We stop and smell it—breathe deep. Terry tells me how when he used to rock climb he liked the smell of lichens on the rubber soles of his shoes. "We used to sit around and talk about how much we liked that smell."

We figure it's an hour back to the truck, so we slow down even more. The dog is impatient and trots ahead, waiting at each curve to make sure we are still moving. We have finally slowed down to what a friend of mine calls the speed of life. All the classes, interstates, and responsibilities are far away. We've got the rest of the day. Then a woman running the trail seriously, at road-race clip, passes us. She is young and strong in running shorts and Lycra top; she is focused straight ahead; she leads a black dog on a leash; three minutes behind, another woman passes, struggling with her breathing, stumbling along the trail, but somehow almost keeping up with the faster woman ahead. They are probably out for an early morning six-mile run. Probably under fifty minutes. They are like ghosts of the world out there running past. Like lightning bolts from another century, as strange to me as the Scout troop the night before with the orange headgear.

"That doesn't look like much fun for the woman behind," Terry says.

"They were probably at Lick Log Creek twenty minutes ago," I say.

Before we're out of the deeper woods, the trail narrows, and we walk through a long alley of Carolina hemlocks. Stands of hemlocks were not logged until more recently. "Formally spared the ax," *Peterson's Field Guide to Eastern Trees* explains, "because of the poor quality of the wood and the stone-like hardness of the knots, which will chip steel blades." Now the trees are "taken for pulp" and for the bark, "rich in tannin." A tea, the field guide says, was made from the leaves and twigs by "Indians and woodcutters," and "seeds and needles [are] eaten by ruffed and sharp-tailed grouse and red squirrels."

The stand makes a less practical, more aesthetic impact on us. The light makes crossing shadows on the trail. It's the best kind of woodlands moment, magic and mysterious. The soil is deep and dark around us. The hemlocks are tall and mature. Terry stops and says, "Listen to the wind. The wind just barely ticks a little. Tiny pops."

I listen. I hear crows in the distance, and a few songbirds, and finally I hear what Terry is talking about. The wind barely moving through the trees. Then Terry looks down, noticing something else, the forest floor. "Humus layers are successive forest floors. One on top of another. So when you are looking at a patch of ground you're dealing in three dimensions—shadows and light. But then, no, four dimensions if you add time. Hear the cars? It's hard to get away from them."

Terry's observations are similar to the sort that Ed Gentry is capable of in *Deliverance*. It's the main reason I love to reread the book. Time slows down enough in the novel's narrative that Ed begins to notice things—smells, sights, sounds. He enters the river and the forest in all its singular presence. Dickey often parallels Ed's sharp senses and his feeling of the world's presence with danger. When Ed has to decide what to do with the rapist that Lewis has shot, he says, "I listened to the woods and the river to see if I could get an answer." Near the end of the novel, when Ed climbs the cliff to stalk the escaped local, the presumed killer of Drew, he's at his most observant. He's at the "end of his rope," and all he has left is the dark cliff in front of him.

What do our sharp observation and understanding add to our lives? What do we bring back from a weekend in the woods intended to deliver us? I leave these questions still unanswered as we hike on toward the parking lot at Russell Bridge.

When we get back to the floodplain, just before we reach the parking lot, it's quiet. All we can hear is the river and the cars along Highway 28. All the campers are gone. They've packed up and left the river to us outsiders. "It *is* Sunday morning. Home for church services probably," Terry says. I remember how Don Belt had described the "Chattooga Country" people years earlier in a 1983 *National Geographic* article: "a straight-faced, Bible-reading people, fearsome in anger, and exceedingly slow to forgive . . . folks who will do anything in the world for you except give up their pride."

We toss our packs in the back of the truck and load the dog, head back toward Walhalla and the other world. Along the way the parking lots are still full of Sunday worshippers at a dozen rural churches.

"Fishing's one thing in these hills, but God's another matter," I say. The ritual of every Sunday's service. The coming of spring. The longer days and shorter nights. Light's deliverance, triumph over darkness, some might say. Others turn their ear to the river like Ed Gentry, listening deeply for the rising water of spring run-off and flood.

Easy Water

SECTION II

FROM

LONG BOTTOM

FORD TO

EARL'S FORD

What I wanted was to float

my piece of the river again.

JOHN GRAVES

Good-bye to a River

CLOSING IN ON NOON it's becoming obvious that Watts Hudgins's friend Matt has stood us up. It's the river runner's nightmare: establish a long-distance shuttle—two cars from two separate cities—and the second car doesn't show. We've done all we can to give Matt some extra time, unloaded the kayak and the canoe in a misting, early spring rain, discussed the possibilities for delay or abandonment—girlfriend problems, car trouble, an accident. Finally we've walked down to the Chattooga and filled Mike Tindall, a first-timer on white water, with a few frightening stories concerning how water, boats, and humans can collide on the twenty-eight miles of the Chattooga River below Russell Bridge.

No other boaters are using the launch site at Long Bottom Ford this day. Watts stops at the river's edge with the canoe, says he likes the water level and he likes the solitude. He's rail thin, dark haired, and dressed in vintage outdoor clothing. His red Patagonia fleece is probably a decade old. He's in his early thirties, almost twenty years younger than I am, but we share the same paddling aesthetic. Neither of us has made the leap to the new, tiny "play boats," and we're proud of it in some strange, reactionary way.

A lover of adventure sports from a young age, Watts began paddling and rock climbing at Camp Pinnacle in the mountains of North Carolina when he was a teen and has since kayaked many of the most difficult and wild white-water rivers in the Southeast and beyond—Gauley, New, Nantahala, Nolichucky, Ocoee, Obed, Youghiogeny, Cheat, even the Colorado through the Grand Canyon.

As Watts begins the litany of his past adventures on the Chattooga, I realize that there are probably a thousand boaters out there in the Southeast like us—men and women who gained their white-water stripes on the Chattooga and still return to her for recreation and repose. The "war story," as recounting near misses has come to be called, is a part of every paddling trip.

The three of us stand watching the river flow. The day has warmed up a little, but it's still cool, in the low fifties. Watts keeps glancing toward the parking lot, checks over his gear, stuffing a few things in a dry bag. He tells Mike about his first frightening run down Five Falls, the quarter-mile series of Class IV and V rapids almost thirty miles downstream.

"When I first paddled Section IV, I was drifting below the Highway 76 bridge and I realized it was too late to abort the trip," he says. "About the time we got to Surfing Rapid, the bridge disappeared upstream. I was on the intimidating 'river of death,' a push up from anything I'd done before."

I tell a similar story of my first trip down Section IV. "I swam at the bottom of the first falls, Entrance Rapid, and missed my roll. Corkscrew, one of the most difficult and dangerous rapids on the river, was just below," I explained. "I grabbed onto John Pilley's kayak as we drifted toward the rapid. 'Let go of my boat. You're on your own,' Pilley said as I slipped toward the edge."

Mike looks a little anxious, although he knows enough about the river to realize he doesn't have to worry about Corkscrew today. Though a novice on white-water rivers, Mike's no stranger to water. He spent a stint in the Navy, submarines. With his uncertainty about what awaits him in the "wilds" of South Carolina, Mike's like a character right out of *Deliverance,* more the introspective Ed Gentry or sensitive Drew Ballinger than Bobby Trippe or Lewis Medlock. When we picked him up outside Greenville, Mike's wife gave Watts specific instructions not to put her husband in harm's way. Watts assured her that the Chattooga's Section II is plenty calm enough for a novice and not to worry. "The bottom doesn't fall out until you get on Section III below Earl's Ford," I say as we stand next to the river and point out white-water features such as waves and eddies on the moving surface of the river.

The Chattooga Section II is perfect for Mike's initiation to the river—"an ideal training run for beginning white-water boaters," one of the guidebooks calls it. It's seven miles of calm, clear water punctuated with easy shoals and only one Class III rapid. It's also a good stretch for fans of wild rivers like Watts and me.

A river can bore neither of us. We're among the lovers of rivers. "I think a river is the most beautiful thing in nature," James Dickey said in an interview in 1970, the same year the novel came out. "*Any* river."

Any stretch of the Chattooga proves Dickey right. Though there is little in the way of white-water challenge or adventure for an advanced boater on this stretch, I know that soon after the river departs the road downstream from the Long Bottom Ford put-in, we'll float through a wide valley farmed for a thousand years, first by the Native Americans and later by hardy settlers such as the Russell family. The old fields are now in succession, and the protected trees have reached impressive size in the Wild and Scenic River corridor.

Soon as we float out of the valley, the river's character will change. A mile or so downstream it's more wild than scenic, the classic gorge profile begins to emerge, and this topography continues virtually unbroken for almost thirty miles.

"This trip's like a little Chattooga sampler," I tell Mike. "It'll introduce you to what you might experience below on future trips."

Mike nods, and you can tell he's thinking about the river and what sort of challenges it offers. Watts looks upstream, and I mention hiking above Russell Bridge. Watts fills Mike in about the rules for use above our put-in. He explains how the West Fork—Sections II, III, and IV—offer the only boating on the protected sections of the river.

I've always liked the symmetry of the current rules concerning use on the river. Legally, here at Long Bottom Ford is where the boating of the Chattooga can begin. The wild and scenic experience of the beautiful, benign Section II is the initiation passage. Just above the Highway 28 bridge, fines are levied for dropping a boat in the moving current or running the numerous waterfalls upstream through the headwaters. Only fishermen and hikers fording the river are welcome, though renegade boaters in pursuit of new adventure occasionally do risk the fines to run the forbidden Chattooga above the bridge.

Deep in me there is person who likes established limits and respects them. I could spend the rest of my life paddling the three familiar sections of the Chattooga below Russell Bridge and never feel boxed in or cheated. The whole boating community doesn't feel this way though. In recent years there has been an active organized effort to open brave new worlds of white water all across the country. The headwaters of the Chattooga are one of the hot spots for these efforts.

In recent years the American Whitewater Association has fought for access to these upper stretches now restricted only to fishing. The right to float a particular river, especially if the river is public land, is what AWA believes is really at issue in opening the headwaters to private boating. Because of concern from citizens' groups like AWA, the Forest Service is considering amendments to its Sumter National Forest Land and Resource Management Plan concerning boating access in the headwaters.

Though it is called Wild and Scenic, the Chattooga is defined in terms of a series of complex legal and legislative documents—congressional acts; national, state, and local laws; standard management practices of organizations such as the Forest Service; amendments;

regulations. Though the river exists as a flood of documents in Washington, this morning it also runs clear and strong next to the boat ramp. I'll take some comfort in my contrary nature today. When we finally get on the water I'll slip into the river and finally forget all the complex issues of boater access.

Even if the amendment is accepted by the Forest Service, boating would be limited, AWA argues, by low water levels on the river most of the year, forming natural barriers to extensive use. The organization also argues "boater use is consistent with law and policy, whereas the prohibition is not."

The conflict has become more pronounced as advances in whitewater equipment and training have made vertical upstream streambeds—once unthinkable for recreational river running but now commonplace—enticing. Young paddlers who would have once been considered hair boaters (daredevil kayakers willing to risk life and limb for a thrill) are now comfortable on steep creeks like the headwaters of the Chattooga. If it's runnable and public land, why not run it? That's their argument.

There's nothing upstream I want to run, but I have to remember that when I show up at a put-in with a beat-up wooden paddle and a ten-year-old, out-of-production kayak I'm considered a living history exhibit.

It's after one in the afternoon and Watts has lost patience with waiting. He decides he'll set the shuttle himself and hitchhike back to where we will wait at the put-in. The misting rain continues.

"Matt's got a red pickup," Watts yells as he drives off in his Toyota. He's headed downstream to Earl's Ford, where he'll drive the Forest Service road to the remote take-out parking lot and leave the Toyota. He'll then jog a mile or so back out to the pavement if there isn't anyone there to offer a ride back to the put-in for Section II. I know we've got a half-hour wait if Watts's luck is good, maybe as much as two hours if his luck is bad.

Mike's not sure what's going on. He doesn't really know me (he's

Watts's friend, a former coworker at a computer company in Greenville), and we've got his head spinning with the entire lingo of put-ins and take-outs and what's downstream. It's his canoe that he and Watts will paddle down, but floating rivers is new to him. The Mohawk canoe has traversed only a few up-country lakes. I break the silence after Watts has left by telling him an embarrassing story about taking a carload of young women on the Chattooga once. When we arrived at Earl's Ford, one of them asked, "Is this where we put out?"

This story, part of my own personal river lore, loosens Mike up. Soon he's talking about John Prine, even singing a few lyrics. We're leaning against the supports of the aging, brown Forest Service kiosk, whose roof is made of cedar shakes, trying to stay dry, when a red pickup drives into the empty parking area. "That might be Matt," Mike says, but I can see that this truck's got a lockbox in the bed. No racks and no boat. We watch as the truck parks, and a very large man steps out. Mike glances at me for some sign as to the right customs in dealing with strangers in *Deliverance* country.

The man walks over to talk. "Gonna rain on you today," he states as way of introduction. He's wearing a brown hat that says "duck hunter" with a little caricature of Daffy Duck. Both his forearms have full-body tattoos of naked ladies. We ask how he's doing and he says he's just out riding around. He's from down near Sumter, South Carolina, and he's up for the weekend at his place up in Long Creek, near the take-out for Section III. "I've got ten acres backing up to the Forest Service land. I'm in the woods. It looks just like that," he says pointing across the highway into the thick second-growth forest. "You can't see my place from the road. I even painted it brown."

"I looked for some land up here but couldn't ever find any to suit me," I said.

Mike's taking it all in, and he seems relieved the conversation has veered toward something as familiar as real estate.

"Me and my wife—she passed on two years ago—used to come

up here all the time to fish and camp. We got to know the locals and always asked if anyone knew of land for sale. After a few years somebody finally told me about somebody with some. I got ten acres, five hundred dollars an acre. I pulled a trailer on it until my brother-in-law could get down from Pennsylvania and build me a house. He finally got down and framed a twenty-seven-foot addition around my trailer. Soon as I get a porch on the front and back I'll be finished."

"Sounds like you got a good deal," I say.

"Well, the local people got to get to know you, but soon as they do, they'll let you in."

"You fishing today?" Mike asks.

"Told my brother-in-law I'd drive down here and see if they were biting. He wants to take three days and come down. He won't come if they're not biting."

"Well, there were eight or nine cars at the trailhead," I add.

"Up at the Georgia line?" the man asks. "Maybe they're biting," he adds. "I ought to be getting on with it."

A few minutes after the fishing scout leaves in his red pickup, headed off on his mission, Watts pulls up in a silver Jeep Cherokee with tinted windows. The passenger window slowly rolls down and a platinum-haired lady says, "You ought to keep up with him better." Watts opens the back door and steps out, thanks his ride, and they laugh and raise mixed drinks they are nursing and drive away.

"They were drinking martinis," Watts says, shaking his head. "When we drove into the parking lot they got one look at you two and said, 'With those beards you better be glad you didn't send those two out to get a ride.'"

We finally go down to the river's edge, gear up for the float, strapping on PFDs (personal flotation devices) over paddling jackets, and push off from the boat launch. We start downstream in what, for now, is still a light rain. It's after two by the time we get on the water. I'm a little worried about the time. Though it's not too cold now, I know that the heat of the day has passed. By the time we get off the river late in the afternoon it will be much cooler. For now I'm snug and comfortable in my Acadia touring kayak equipped with a lightweight nylon spray skirt. Watts and Mike are behind me in their forest green canoe, an open boat. I look back as Mike puts on his wide-brimmed straw hat, and with his long, black beard he looks Amish, an Amish farmer out for a Saturday float.

Though I am ahead of them, I can hear Watts going through all the strokes that might be new to our novice river paddler, the draw, the crossbow draw, the pry, the rudder. The camp counselor in Watts has emerged with a vengeance, a good thing since Mike will need to know a few strokes to negotiate several of the rapids on this stretch.

I drift, my bow headed upstream, and listen to Watts's stroke drill from a distance. Over the winter, when I'm often away from the river, I always forget how comfortable it is seeing a canoe float on moving water. The sleek lines are perfect and practical and define the craft against the backdrop of low, misty hills.

The gaudy colors and shapes of most kayaks (my boat is bright blue) add a high-tech, purely recreational element to floating that I have to admit I have conflicted feelings about. "An unadventurous boat, of retrospective design," is how Franklin Burroughs describes his old canoe in *The River Home,* a contemporary narrative that describes his float down the Waccamaw River in the low country of the Carolinas. As we float through the long river bottom, which was once a field of corn, I realize that he's right about a canoe. The very shape harkens back to boats designed for carrying a load.

The load I carry this morning is mostly memory. My memories are clustered around the theme of descent, and I let them carry me into the mist and rain. Years ago, in the early 1990s, there was a festival on the Chattooga, and rafting teams came from all over the world to run one leg of a white-water rally on the river. The teams from the Soviet Union (it was right before the Union fell apart) impressed me with their homemade equipment. Every raft looked like something Robinson Crusoe would have pasted together from available materials. There was one wild craft with two huge rubber tubes like doughnuts lashed together with saplings. The two paddlers rolled it to the river and launched it, bouncing into the current.

I glance down at my own high-tech plastic flat-water kayak. Eight hundred fifty dollars at your local outfitter's store. There's too much money in paddling today. The gear has been transformed by the same market forces that took over skiing decades ago—designers want the gear to appeal to a young adventurous crowd and they make it performance ready—high speed, lightweight, and flashy. Fashion now has as much to do with paddling as practicality. Many boats cost over one thousand dollars, but they are obsolete the moment new models hit the market. Clothes are expensive, crafted of synthetic materials that often were developed for the space program. I'll admit the new gear is warmer and dryer, but I wonder whether my real comfort level is greatly increased by the new advances.

In the old days we wore wool sweaters bought on the cheap from Salvation Army stores and clumsy neoprene wet suits designed for diving. My real comfort as I float along comes from knowing that we're on a section of the river where we're not likely to see any of the new paddlers. I won't be reminded of the way paddle sports have evolved.

Several hard forward strokes bring me back to the river and help me forget about my gear. After all, the boat is little more than a vehicle. The float's the thing, I remind myself.

"Put on the river / Like a fleeing coat," James Dickey implored me in college when I discovered the lines of his poem "Inside the River" from the collection *Drowning with Others*. "Move with the world." I dip my hand in the current, the water forming a glove up to my wrist. The coat will have to wait for a warmer day.

Has anyone written more beautifully about water and our relationship to it than James Dickey? In his poetry there is a crystal essence glimpsed occasionally in the prose of *Deliverance*.

I paddle up next to Watts and Mike, and a little discussion ensues as to where the West Fork of the Chattooga enters the river. I think that we will pass it just downstream. Watts remembers that it enters above where we put in, a hundred yards or so downstream from Russell Bridge, flowing in from the Georgia side. Glancing at a map, if we had one, would have answered this question.

A river is formed of numerous tributaries, and the West Fork of the Chattooga, wherever it may be, is one of its largest. *Deliverance*'s director, John Boorman, used this fork to portray Dickey's mythical wild Cahulawassee in its calmer upper reaches. It's the last of the three forks to merge and form the main river. The famous scene where the banjo boy watches the four suburban adventurers float below him was shot upstream on the West Fork.

A four-mile stretch of the West Fork offers good boating. The put-in is upstream at Overflow Road campground. It's a small stream, only thirty to fifty feet wide in places, and the current is slow with several small shoals and two Class II rapids, Dam Sluice and Big Slide.

In 1997 two developers purchased 229 acres along the West Fork, a parcel known locally as the Nicholson Tract, and attempted to close the river to public access. They stretched a cable across the current and suspended a sign that said Absolutely No Trespassing Survivors Will Be Prosecuted, attempting to close two miles of the river through their property. Though the sign was threatening in itself, the landowners also positioned themselves onshore and demanded that paddlers stop before they entered their property and that they leave the river.

The legal system went to work. Environmental lawyers argued that the landowners couldn't stop anyone from using the river. There were twenty-five years of use as a precedent. The landowners cited property rights. "If I catch anybody out there, we'll take them to jail," one of the developers said in a news story. "I own the land on both sides of the river and the land beneath the water. Of course, I don't own the water." They reported that they wanted to develop a golf course and residential housing on their tract of land, one of the last large tracts of private land within the Wild and Scenic River corridor.

One of the owners reported he'd be thrilled to work out a deal with the Forest Service. "The developers come in, buy these scenic areas, and hold the property to extort big bucks from the federal government," Buzz Williams told the local media.

The Chattooga Conservancy (formally the Chattooga River Watershed Coalition) has been involved in the issue of public land acquisition since it was founded in 1991. Buzz and his organization see acquisition as their mission as it enhances "for posterity those areas which have unique biological, cultural, geological, or recreational values." In their first decade of operation, CRWC worked with members of Congress and with land trusts to buy land from willing sellers. Unfortunately, the price of land in the watershed has jumped and it is becoming difficult to acquire the remaining key tracts of private land. The Nicholson Tract, where developers were trying to stop access on the river, was always one of the key tracts.

When the sign went up, tempers flared. Paddlers and fishing enthusiasts were denied access to the river. The story spread quickly throughout the region. The West Fork story drew heavy media coverage. Local and regional papers wrote about the standoff. For two weeks the river was closed. CNN finally showed up, but found that the sign had been changed to read For Sale, with a number displayed to call for more information. Many felt that the landowners had shrewdly used the media coverage to advertise.

It was reported that the owners had purchased the tract for 1.5 million dollars. Their asking price by the time CNN became involved was 3.8 million. The Forest Service was able to reestablish public access to the river with a temporary restraining order, and soon after that, the Office of General Counsel and the U.S. Attorney argued the status of the West Fork as a navigable waterway. This assured the case for public access.

The story has a happy ending. In 2000 an Atlanta businessman purchased the tract from the landowners and sold it to the Conservation Fund. They held the land until 2001 when the Forest Service acquired funds so that the land could pass into permanent public ownership.

What now? A use and management plan for the tract is being

developed. Some of the land is floodplain spotted with open fields. There are some poorly built logging roads as well. The Chattooga Conservancy would like to see the roads rehabilitated, along with the native ecosystems of the tract. Native cane and native trees (possibly including American Chestnut) could be planted. Buzz thinks native brook trout could be reintroduced if work is done to improve water quality through stream-bank restoration.

Whether the Forest Service will focus on restoring and preserving native ecosystems as Buzz and the Chattooga Conservancy would prefer is yet to be settled. Restoration is still both a politically and biologically contested issue. It's expensive and varies with many of the typical management practices used in other areas of the local national forests.

I wish Buzz and the conservancy luck. Though no ecologist, I feel sympathy for restoration and a natural disposition toward difficult (and often expensive) solutions.

After a few minutes it's obvious Watts is right and the confluence with the West Fork was above us, before the put-in. As we float downstream, I tip my paddle in the upstream direction of the West Fork toward that not-so-long-ago skirmish between the two developers and all those who love the Chattooga for reasons besides personal profit.

Our profit today is entirely internal and hard to gauge. There is no adrenaline to contend with and not one hard decision to be made. Section II would be the perfect float for the blind. It's all sound and sense. Drifting along we're "recreating," what the Wild and Scenic River document calls "the main attraction of the Chattooga River." We're exercising our right to visit this river and "experience solitude, adventure, and challenge." I think back to *Deliverance* and confirm my kinship to Lewis, Dickey's outdoor enthusiast morphed forever by the magic of Hollywood into Burt Reynolds in a sleeveless wet-suit top. "We ought to go up there before the real estate people get hold of it and make it over into one of their heavens," Lewis drawls at the novel's outset.

Moments after my reverie, we float beside a small house on the shore. You don't have to paddle down the West Fork to see real estate, private rather than public property. Within the first mile downstream from the put-in on Section II there are four river cottages along a small secondary road that runs parallel to Highway 28. These are the only houses along the entire length of the Chattooga, inholdings that the Forest Service didn't or couldn't buy when the Wild and Scenic River corridor was established in 1974. They are mostly jerry-built affairs that have been casually maintained for years. They have that handmade-house look, gray, aging rough-cut lumber, sagging porches, broken panes of glass, nothing plumb, and three or four rooms cantilevered out at odd angles.

On the first one we float past there's a cheap stovepipe protruding at an impossible angle. Against the empty front porch of the second, only a dozen feet from the river, an old mop leans, abandoned there after fall cleaning or in anticipation of a spring scrubbing. These cottages grow like mushrooms out of the duff under the mountain laurel and rhododendron. Downstream the scream of a Skilsaw and the percussion of a nail gun announce that someone is adding on to their little cottage in paradise. As we pass we see that they have continued the tradition of their neighbors and the new room looks temporary.

These inholdings remind me that even something as appreciated as the Wild and Scenic River corridor is still politically contested. The legislation often runs up against the deep-seated issue of property rights. Who owns this rich, lovely landscape? There is no doubt these four river cottages predate the establishment of the corridor in 1974, and somehow they have survived it and their owners have continued to enjoy their river in the old ways of their ancestors. These are not cottages built by rich vacationers. They are local getaways. Wendell Berry writes beautifully about his uncle's Kentucky River shack in *The Long-Legged House*. Rivers have always drawn such characters as Berry's uncle and there's a part of me that respects the persistence of dreams of living on the river.

The four shacks we pass are a perfect contrast to the Russell family homestead just upstream, where a Carolina pioneer family thrived for several centuries. I'm always reminded that the rich bottoms where the West Fork of the Chattooga joins with this, the main trunk, was the site of Chattooga Town, a Cherokee village and jumping-off spot for excursions into the piedmont and on down to the coast. Trails have always crossed the river here, and people have lived for a millennium or longer along this stretch of river.

What is the right way to live with a river? Are farming the river bottoms and seasonally fishing its pools better ways of life than weekend visits by adventurers in plastic boats? It seems the answers escape just downstream each time I have one within reach. The complexities of nature and culture are never easy to sort through, and simple answers always leave someone lost in a patch of cane they thought they knew a clear path through.

The rain begins to fall harder as we leave the cottages behind. It's colder as well. Above us, on the South Carolina side, the steep wooded slopes of Russell Mountain look as if some mad giant has stumbled through, hanging huge gray cotton balls of cloud in all the treetops. "I'll bet half the days I've spent on this river have been overcast like this one," Watts says from the stern of Mike's canoe. All there is to do once we are past the shacks is to watch the river. The surface, dimpled by rain, is still winter gray and humped with hidden rocks under the moving water. Where the river straightens out you can look downstream and see the faint shadow of spring ready to emerge. You can feel the green ready to pop out from the birches and willows along the shore. There are no wildflowers yet—it is only mid-March—but it's no longer deep winter. The air temperature is in the sixties, but even with the rain it doesn't feel cold.

It's quiet on the river, and there is adventure merely being back in its flow. I'll admit it's mostly the excitement that's developed with time. It revolves for me around attention—noticing small things, like how the surface of the slate gray current is pocked by a light rain, how the native hemlocks along the shore absorb the moisture. Their branches hang heavy. I know from other paddling trips that ahead of me the Chattooga is crowded only with mist and the sound of water rolling over stones.

These river miles are slow and beautiful, running through the Wild and Scenic River corridor and national forest on both sides. The river is the dividing line between Sumter National Forest on the South Carolina bank and Chattahoochee National Forest in Georgia. The names of the two forests are so different—Sumter named for Thomas Sumter, "the Gamecock," a Revolutionary War hero from South Carolina's low country. Georgia, on the other hand, offers *Chattahoochee,* the Cherokee word for "river of painted rock" or "river of pounded corn," depending on which source you prefer. Not only the name of a national forest, Chattahoochee is also the name of a sister river to the Chattooga, one watershed south, whose headwaters rise in these familiar mountains of north Georgia.

Off in the woods on the Georgia side (the western bank), the Bartram and Chattooga Trails run as one through the hemlock forest, hugging the rising swell of Willis Knob. The trail is ten miles long and runs from Russell Bridge to Earl's Ford, the entire length of Section II. It's a moderate hike through the forest with a few views of the river. The elevation change is only two hundred feet, so it's a perfect hike for someone who wants to encounter the Chattooga for the first time. There are a couple of creek crossings—Adline Branch, Laurel Branch. These are wet fords, with the cold water often knee-deep, and it's best to know this before one sets out. There are also horse trails on both sides of the river often used by mountain bikers and hikers as well. It's truly a multiuse area.

We stop once and exit our boats for a couple of minutes to stretch and look at a strange, low-water bridge we can see just below the surface of the river. The ghostly remains of the bridge were probably essential infrastructure years ago and offered a farmer access to the last strip of bottomland on the Georgia side of the river. Now a dark, mysterious grove of evergreens fills in the space where corn once grew. As we stretch and look at the gray shadow of the bridge under the river's surface, Watts tells of once hiking through the grove: "There were old tractors, abandoned and rusted in various places, and the trees were all planted in neat, uniform rows, like a tree farm."

I'm colder, and before I get back in the kayak, I peel off my paddling jacket and add one more layer of synthetic fiber that I've stowed away in a dry bag in the bulkhead of the touring kayak. I'm feeling a little like the Michelin Man as my spray skirt pops back into place, but I'd rather be warm than cold on this paddle.

On the Chattooga, weather is a reality, and it moves through like migrating birds. Hypothermia is one of the most serious dangers inherent in paddling. Cold March water and cool moist air make for a deadly combination. Once I took a freshman humanities class on a canoe clinic on this section of the Chattooga in November. What had been a splendid late fall Friday turned nasty overnight, and by the time we were on the water that Saturday morning, the temperatures had dropped below fifty. Our instructors stopped two miles into the trip and started a fire on a beach in order to warm up two students who had turned over their canoe horsing around.

Today a chilly mist is hanging from branches and gathering just above the dark boulders. In spite of this cool day, the year creeps toward spring, and this shows up particularly in the maples, whose red tips hold out the first hint of the leaves waiting to push forth.

I look for other signs of spring high up on the steep slopes of South Carolina's Callas Mountain. I can't see far. The peak is lost in the clouds, and besides, it's still deep winter up there.

The rain distracts me from the river, and I float right through the first Class II, Turn Hole, about three miles downstream from the put-in at Russell Bridge. Rain starts to pick up as we float down and we hear ahead of us the only Class III on this section, a tricky ledge called Big Shoals, a boulder pile with no apparent path through. Up ahead of me, Watts and Mike beach their canoe on a large scouting rock midriver and stand on it. I pull up and get out. Watts points out how he would like to run the rapid, left of the rock they're standing on. I look at the route. Most of the water is going right, but I see what Watts is avoiding. There's a bad undercut rock on the right side. The run there would demand a little more technical maneuvering than Watts thinks Mike is ready for this early in his white-water career.

The rain falls harder as we explain the options to Mike. It's an easy portage if that's what he prefers—just bang the canoe over the ledge and get back in below. We decide to run, choosing the left route. Watts points out to Mike that even if they flip there's a big calm pool below the ledge and the take-out can't be more than a couple of miles downstream, so they won't be wet long. Mike looks down at the rushing water and says he is ready to add this Class III rapid to the adventures of the day.

We all slip back into our boats and run the rapid easily. Everybody does fine, and Mike is thrilled by the excitement of his first real white water. As we sit in the pool at the bottom, Watts notes that they have taken some water on the descent through the rapid. They head for shore to flip the canoe. After the Chattooga drains from their boat back into the river, Watts says, "Forward," and sticks his canoe paddle into the rain. We slip back into the current.

The canoe doesn't stay dry for long. The late winter rain turns into a tumult as we float downstream toward Earl's Ford, the Section II take-out. The mist is so thick the hemlocks disappear among floating swales of fog. The fingers of dense green foliage puncture the space over the river.

We pass through Five Ledges, the only other named rapid on Section II, in a pelting rain. The clouds are low and the river is covered with tiny gray impacts from the pellets of rain.

I'm cold, I think. Damned cold. I wonder how Watts and Mike are faring in their canoe. Through the driving rain I can make out Mike's wide-brimmed hat. It's soaked and the brim slumps down around his face. It looks like one of those funnel hats worn in rice paddies. Watts has pulled out a black neoprene beanie he sometimes wears under his kayak helmet and he looks like some sort of rescued fighter pilot slumped in the canoe's stern. We look desperate. We're on the easiest section of the Chattooga, out for a Sunday afternoon paddle, and somehow things have turned scary. The story starts to sound a little too familiar. Drew's *Deliverance* ghost begins to tap-dance like the rain on the bow of my kayak.

I watch the South Carolina side for anything that looks like a take-out. I can see that Watts is doing the same. Mike keeps his head down, stroke after stroke. Mike may be the most relaxed of the three of us. He doesn't have to make any decisions. He's counting on the knowledge that the two veteran Chattooga river runners are supposed to possess.

I see what could be a trail coming down to the river. The run-off from the storm pours into the river from the opening in the trees. Is this a gully or a trail? Surely we've paddled far enough to get off this river. The banks and river and sky all start to merge into a wet fuzzy shoal of gray. Without rapids to mark our passage it's hard to figure how much progress we've made. Is this Earl's Ford? Is this stretch of river five miles or seven miles? These questions float into my mind as I scan the South Carolina bank for any sign of a trail.

I know what Earl's Ford looks like. There's a big sandbar and a road on the Georgia side right down to the river. A distinctive creek, Warwoman, comes in from the Georgia side. In my right mind it would be impossible to mistake this take-out, a spot I've used as a put-in for Section III scores of times. But I'm not in my right mind. All the heat is leaving me and my mind is more jelly than flesh. The worm of doubt is eating my confidence about trails and trailheads and take-outs. It's late in the afternoon, pouring rain, and darkness crouches like some avenger in the forest duff.

It thunders. The misting rain has now turned to thunderstorm. The thunder rolls down the river like a bowling strike in God's alley. In a minor panic I pull over and pop my spray skirt and shoulder my kayak and start humping up the first trail that is really a trail. Watts and Mike follow me over to the take-out, pop out, and drag the canoe inland. I'm shaking with a chill. We carry our boats up the trail in the pouring rain. I know this doesn't look like Earl's Ford, but I don't really care. I just want to be off the river. I want to leave the ghost of *Deliverance* in the moving current and driving rain. I want to enter the warm Subway in Westminster, South Carolina, and add this war story to all the others. I want to laugh about how stupid we all were, how close we were to that demon hypothermia. I want hot coffee.

After ten minutes of slipping and sloshing inland and uphill on what we all three decide is a horse trail (liquid horse droppings underfoot) we finally stop for a moment and realize we've been paralleling the river since we left it. "We're headed back upstream to Russell Bridge," Watts says. Without saying any more we turn back and head for the river. "Thunder or no thunder, we'll float some more," Watts says getting back in the canoe. "If we come upon the Narrows, we'll know we've gone way too far."

No shit, I think as Watts makes his joke. The Narrows is the second Class IV rapid on Section III, three miles downstream from Earl's Ford. If we do indeed make it to the Narrows, there will be no doubt in my mind we've entered some black hole that's deposited us unknowing in the middle of a low-budget film script.

We make one more false start, this time hauling our boats through the woods, and come out on a gravel road, look around in the rain, and decide we have no idea where we are. Mike stays calm. He's followed us up two trails, two soaked, spooked Marco Polos, and he's not about to give up now. We are Mike's only hope. We are each other's hope as well. Watts appraises the situation and says, "I think we're close. Let's paddle down just a little further."

There hasn't been another crack of thunder since the first one. Somehow there's enough blood flowing to Watts's brain for him to be reflective: "In my mind this section of river is five miles long. I think now it was probably seven. As we got into the last two miles I started getting ready for a take-out. I'm a little embarrassed," he says as an apology to Mike. "Never did I ever imagine I would approach hypothermia on Section II."

We reenter the river. I sprint off, using solid forward strokes to accelerate, to warm myself, feeling a new sense of purpose. Watts and Mike fall in line. The rain has let up a little, and I'm not quite so cold. We float up to the actual Earl's Ford take-out, and it all comes back to me. I realize there's no way we could have passed this take-out. It's as obvious as any landmark on this familiar river. When we're in sight of the take-out—sandbar on the left and creek on the right—I look back at Watts and Mike following a dozen yards behind me in the canoe. I want to pump my fist in air like Ed Gentry at the end of *Deliverance*, but I resist. It's a much smaller triumph. Instead I simply take a big wide sweep stroke, head my boat toward South Carolina, and beach it in the sand.

Pilley's Perfect River

SECTION III

FROM

EARL'S FORD

TO

SANDY FORD

I took a rock and released it into

the waters of a better world.

DAVID JAMES DUNCAN

The River Why

GROUP OF US IS PADDLING from Earl's Ford to Sandy
Ford with John Pilley, soon after his seventieth birthday. It's mid-
September, ninety degrees, and everyone in our group wants a cold
front to push some tolerable air into the southeast. As we began our
float, I dip my hands in the Chattooga's current. The water is cool,
holding the chill from the higher mountain thirty miles north.

It hasn't rained in weeks, so the river's level is down to half a
foot. The moss on the rocks, usually close to water level, is stranded
high, dry and dead. Drought and flood are the landscape's vengeful
sisters, and they each can grip this river forcefully. As I swing into
the diminished current I admit that I prefer flood, exuberance, and
the danger that comes from the river near its capacity. Flood though
is only a spike, an event that quickly passes, enduring for no more
than a day or so. Droughts linger, defined by a drop in precipitation
over time. This year we're down eleven inches of rain, down a total
of thirty over the last three years. Who knows how long this one
we're in will last?

Drought conditions make me notice more. The river becomes

secondary to the banks as water drops and channels up. Flood charges me and all I notice is the flow. I checked the gauge on the Internet this morning before meeting Pilley for the drive over. Half a foot was all the water we had, close to a historic low. The skinny river barely has enough water to carry us downstream. Sometimes when we beach on a cobble of round river rocks, it seems as if it would make more sense to hike the three miles from here to Sandy Ford.

But we paddle on. There are other things to see on a Wild and Scenic River, other chemicals in our body besides adrenaline. We follow an American egret down the first mile of river after the put-in. I've never seen an egret on the river. Great blue herons, yes, and often little green herons. But this white bird with the yellow legs is more something I am used to seeing in salt marshes on the coast. It isn't exactly exotic, but the bird, like us, seems an outsider.

The group I have assembled for Pilley's birthday is high-spirited, even though the river is low. There are five of us on the trip whom Pilley has taught to paddle—Tom Langston, a builder near Spartanburg; Lee Hagglund and Alliston Reid, who teach with us at Wofford; and Raymond Curry, a computer salesman. My friends Lilace Mellin and Jimmy Guignard are also along, down from Cullowhee, North Carolina. They don't really know Pilley or the Pilley legend, so as we float down I fill them in, tell my favorite Chattooga stories from my fifteen years paddling with Pilley. Alliston, Lee, Tom, and Raymond add theirs as well.

"Pilley took me down this river on my twenty-first birthday—and he nearly killed me. It was my first trip down Section IV. Late summer," Alliston says as we all sit in the eddy below the first rapid, Warwoman Shoals, just downstream from Earl's Ford. "I paddled through Entrance Rapid fine, but in Corkscrew, I ate it. I came out of my boat and started floating toward Left Crack. Anyway, I lunged for Pilley's grab loop and he pulled me over. I came so close to the crack that I almost wet my pants."

There's nothing in Warwoman Shoals this day to suggest the power of the white water downstream. At normal water levels Warwoman, a Class III named for the mythic Cherokee war leader, is a twisting ride down over two ledges with a powerful eddy at the bottom. Often a down tree blocks the current as well. It's a good place to judge the skill of first-time Chattooga paddlers like Jimmy, but today it's an easy drop with no real push. I watch from the eddy at the bottom as Jimmy follows Lilace through easily.

"My most vivid memory of Pilley is the first time he took me down the section of the river just downstream from here," Lee adds as we drift along. "We got to Dick's Creek Ledge and I did that okay. The Narrows, okay. And as you know, right below the Narrows is Second Ledge. Well, I'd memorized the sequence of rapids and I knew something big was coming. Pilley just said, 'Don't worry, we'll just go right and then work our way back left. I was scared out of my mind. We get over to river left and Pilley says, 'See that rooster tail. That's where you go over.' Then he wheeled his kayak and disappeared."

Lilace and Jimmy listen quietly as we float downstream telling our Chattooga stories. I'm wondering what they're thinking of all the crash and burn. Lilace is a graceful paddler, brown hair under her helmet, tall and slender. I've talked with her about paddling and know she is one of the most reflective of my white-water tribe. "When I'm paddling I'm moving in three planes—earth (rock, bank), water, and air," she explained to me once. "The way the three intersect each other blows my mind out of its ordinary complacency."

Jimmy is tall and strong, a graduate student in literature at Western Carolina University. This is his first time on the river. He's been in a boat a half-dozen times on the Nantahala and the Tuckasegee, two rivers known as beginner water. He has that look in his eye of one not quite sure what's downstream. I try to assure him that the river's so low he has nothing to worry about. Lilace does the same. He doesn't say, but I know he's feeling that first-time-Chattooga thing. This river has such a reputation that, no matter what you are told about it, you have to experience the river yourself to understand.

We approach a small rapid, and the war stories stop as we all float through the three or four small ledges barely covered by current.

Lilace and Jimmy are climbers as well, and I have often heard them compare and contrast the two sports. Jimmy, the novice paddler, is still uncertain of his strokes, even in the shallow water. He is thinking about every move. Climbers, by nature, are more reflective than paddlers. Maybe it's the pace their discipline demands, and the obvious consequences of failing to think moves through. "Climbing narrows my focus," Lilace said once, describing why she was not an adrenaline paddler. "Me, my breath, movements, the rock. Paddling expands my awareness like I imagine hallucinogenic drugs do. I had to deal with a lot of fear in my pursuit of being a better paddler."

The low water is finally giving Jimmy confidence, and he surfs endlessly on a small wave behind one ledge. The rest of the group floats through, and I linger for a few minutes with Lilace as Jimmy practices his boat control. Lilace is comfortable on the Chattooga, a confidence gained through more than a few river trips at many water levels. She says she even dated a river guide for a while. She calls the Chattooga "a testosterone river" and admits being a little uncomfortable with the culture such a place creates. She says that the culture soured her from ever "checking out" on the river in her days as a raft guide. I know that checking out on the Chattooga is the process of learning the river well enough to guide raft trips down, and it is a badge of honor among the staffs of the three rafting companies that have outposts on the river. That Lilace never got that badge keeps her an outsider among the raft guides. Among private boaters there is only one badge of honor, and it is a trip down Section IV. I realize there is a certain macho to our telling stories of our paddling trips and feel a little guilty about it.

Maybe I've stopped to watch Jimmy because I am worried that we—Pilley's band of paddlers—are perpetrating the male stereotype of strength and aggression, one-upping each other with crash-and-burn stories as we float downstream. These stories are the common ground we share, our close calls with the river. It's always a privilege to survive the river and its moods. I have to admit there have been very few women along on these trips. The first ten years of Pilley's career he taught at an all-male school and so his paddlers were usually male.

I don't give away exactly what I'm thinking, but I ask Lilace if she's read *Deliverance.* She says she hasn't read the novel, though she's seen the movie. She laughs and says she likes the movie because it's the only cultural artifact she knows that's made men afraid of being raped. "I think it's fabulous," she says as we watch Jimmy surf, "because culture's always making women feel that way."

I finally ask her what she thinks of all us boys telling our stories. She says she's enjoying it, but admits that it's probably just more of that "male bonding stuff." Knowing Lilace has degrees in literature, I bring up literary critic Donald Greiner's book *Women Enter the Wilderness* and how Greiner, a friend of Dickey's, explores the history of male bonding in American literature, starting with James Fenimore Cooper and continuing through *Deliverance,* a novel Greiner sees as perhaps the last of its kind, a classic story of men entering the wilderness to look for freedom, leaving the women behind. Most of Greiner's book is concerned with novels published since 1980 that have expanded this old theme, culminating with Gloria Naylor's *The Women of Brewster Place,* where a city neighborhood is a "wilderness," and female bonding is explored.

Before Lilace has a chance to respond, Jimmy pops off the wave and floats into the eddy and Lilace takes his place, moving her boat back and forth on the wave with the skill and certainty of an accomplished paddler. From the eddy I ponder my present circumstances— the wild river, my macho disappointment at the diminished flow, the beauty of the small wave Lilace now paddles, and the pleasure, if not excitement, to be found on the river's moving surface.

One feminist critic called *Deliverance,* upon its publication, the "apotheosis of manliness" for American fiction. The critic goes on to describe the landscape of the novel as a territory where "women do not go, where civilization cannot reach, where men hunt one another like animals and hunt animals for sport." The Chattooga Lilace paddles isn't exactly the river Dickey imagines. Lilace is here and she's even comfortable—and now, at the beginning of the twenty-first century, civilization has reached far into our pleasure with permits and advanced boat design, topo maps, and guidebooks. There is no hunting planned on this day trip, though Tom has brought along his fishing rod and plans to wet a hook at lunch.

Is the Chattooga truly a testosterone river as Lilace calls it? I know that some women are among the river's paddling pioneers. Bunny Johns, former president of the Nantahala Outdoor Center, was among the first group of paddlers to descend Section IV in the mid-1950s and has remained a leader in outdoor adventure in the southeast ever since. When Bunny (then Bunny Bergin) made that first trip down Section IV, she was with a group of three men from Camp Merrie-Woode, where she was a canoeing counselor. Several of the men have become legends in southeastern canoeing: Fritz Orr Jr., Al Barrett, and Hugh Caldwell.

The late Hugh Caldwell was a philosophy professor at Sewanee for many years and spent his summers working at summer camps, teaching both girls and boys to canoe. He pioneered many Appalachian rivers as day trips for campers and was probably the first to descend the Chattooga, in 1952. The Section IV trip Bunny was along on was several years later and ended up as quite an adventure, no matter what your gender. The group portaged Woodall Shoals and most of the drops in Five Falls. They lost a fifteen-foot Grumman canoe in Sock-em-Dog, and it never came out of the hole at the rapid's bottom.

Many strands. Many contradictions. That's what makes this a living river. I peel out and head down to catch up with Pilley, Lee, Alliston, Raymond, Tom. I'm not even sure they noticed they've left us behind. I look back over my shoulder and see that Jimmy and Lilace are still alternating playing on the wave, surfing the tiny hole with complete joy. These are two possibilities on the Chattooga—wild river with a challenge and mystery around every bend, and playful beauty spot where time dissolves and bliss rises like a mist.

"She's always got to be respected. She's got her moods, and you have to gauge them every time you approach," Pilley says when I raft up downstream with the other members of our party. I think of the irony of Pilley's choice of metaphor—river as feminine spirit—considering the discussion I've just had with Lilace upstream.

Pilley has often revealed that he thinks of the Chattooga as a woman, one with unpredictable moods. "Water levels on the river do go up and down, much as emotional weather can," I say, trying to agree with Pilley's assessment. "So is the river feminine? It's a question worth pondering."

The water is so low that any distraction gives us something to do as we slowly float and scrape down the river. Nobody bites on my question though. It sinks into the diminished current like a stone. No one defends the gender of the river or offers an alternative.

About a mile downstream from the put-in, we approach Dick's Creek Ledge, the first Class IV on Section III. We can hear the rapid before we see the horizon line marking a significant drop in gradient ahead. Dick's Creek is a river-wide ledge and is only run-nable at lower water levels in the middle, where there is a large dry scouting rock to assess the rapid before committing.

Dick's Creek Ledge has always made my stomach churn, even at low water. It's the type of rapid that makes me remember that kayaking is a skill and not just a roller coaster ride. There's maneuvering to be done while running Dick's Creek, and the wrong paddle stroke can quickly carry you to places you don't want to be. Each time I approach the rapid I remember the one or two worst runs, not the dozens of good ones. I remember the times I've stood on the scouting rock with a rope and seen paddlers miss the difficult S turn and wash over the ledge to land upside down among boulders, and I remember the fear and the lack of control I've felt when I've found myself headed in the same direction. Dick's Creek Ledge is a good thing. It operates as a gatekeeper for those who want a hint of what waits in the more difficult rapids downstream.

We beach our boats there and get out to scout. From our vantage point it's possible to get a good view of Dick's Creek Falls on river right, one of the most impressive waterfalls in the watershed. As one guidebook explains, "The unique combination of a wild waterfall, thundering white water, and the surrounding mountains make this one of the most beautiful scenes on the river."

This dry hot day there is little "thunder," but there is still beauty, and I take it in as I stretch my legs. I look to my left and see that the route through the rapid will not be an easy one. The slide down into an eddy has very little flow, making the approach difficult. It looks more like rock climbing than paddling.

Soon everyone is ready to run Dick's Creek Ledge, so I say that I will stay and wait for Lilace and Jimmy and I'll meet them downstream at our designated lunch spot, a little shoot called Lone Star. I watch from the scouting rock as everyone in the group slips over the drop and scrapes into the S turn, eddies out halfway down, and slips one-by-one through the narrow chute at the bottom. As I watch them go down, I see day hikers wading the river and crossing in front of the waterfall on the Georgia side. As my group scrapes past in their kayaks I can see that the hikers have nothing to worry about today. They are safe from the power of the Chattooga's famous current.

After everyone is safely through the rapid, I look back over my shoulder for Lilace and Jimmy. They are just coming into view. They've had the river to themselves for ten minutes. I watch as they approach and think about how Dick's Creek Ledge is the archetypal Chattooga rapid—a river-wide ledge of resistant bedrock with a recovery pool below that gets more difficult the higher the water. There has even been one death here, in August 1994 in very high water. A tropical storm had passed through and the river had crested that day at ten feet, a flow estimated to be somewhere between a ten- and twenty-five-year flood event. Four inexperienced men had put on in a raft at the Highway 28 bridge, about eleven miles upstream. The raft flipped at Dick's Creek, and a twenty year old drowned, probably in the hydraulic, and his body was found two days later a mile downstream. I imagine for a moment the same look of terror on the faces of the four men. They may have looked as scared and confused as the *Deliverance* characters when they tumbled to their fates over the waterfall toward the end of the movie. I'd bet they'd all seen the scene. At the moment the raft cartwheeled in Dick's Creek's flood-crazed hydraulic, these tourists were living through a terrible reality that mirrored the movie. Three made it to shore. One didn't.

When Lilace and Jimmy beach their boats on the rock, I help them out and tell them it looks like a scrappy run. They listen to my description of the run, look at the S turn and the shallow approach, and decide they both will portage the drop on this day. It's a good decision. I help pull their boats across the narrow passage of rock and on down into the current below. Dick's Creek makes for an easy portage.

I climb back up, snap my spray skirt into place, paddle a few stokes into the approach, and bump down into the S turn, sit for a moment in the eddy between the ledges, wheel and slide through the chute with no problem, and meet Lilace and Jimmy at the bottom.

A short distance below Dick's Creek Ledge, we sit on a slanted boulder above the constricted chute called Lone Star and watch the drought-diminished river flow. When we arrive, it's lunchtime; some have just finished eating sandwiches; some swim in the cooling current. Lilace, Jimmy, and I beach our boats and take out our sandwiches and stretch out on the rocks. "It's a river's river," Lilace notes. No gender there.

"She's a perfect river," I say, just to see how she'll respond.

"No," I correct, thinking of what Pilley had said to me years before on my first paddling trip down the Chattooga, "she's the perfect river." And then add: "Ah, she's the river perfect!"

Of course, I'm thinking of David James Duncan's novel, *The River Why* when I make my pronouncement. Duncan writes of a river in southern Oregon. *The River Why* is quite a kinder, gentler alternative to *Deliverance* as a river story. It's a fishing story, with the main character pulled between his parents, his father a fly fisherman and his mother a bait fisher. There, for Duncan, reality and imagination merge and create a literary landscape more full of questions than answers. The river in Duncan's novel becomes a place of discovery, of psychological power, where Gus, the main character, connects with the landscape through fishing in almost the same way Native Americans do through vision quest.

When I look down at the Chattooga, I look at the real river I love and paddle, but I also see Dickey's mythic southern river that exists only after you read his novel or see the movie. Other southern writers besides Dickey have made up landscapes. Faulkner's Yoknapatawpha County floats like a mirage by the real Oxford and northern Mississippi he inhabited. Places connected to family, community, story, and history have depth.

For almost thirty years the Chattooga has been the perfect answer to hundreds of differing questions asked by paddlers, fishing enthusiasts, and hikers. That is why I agree with Pilley and call the Chattooga the river perfect. What could be more perfect?

Lilace hasn't taken the bait, so I ask her what she thinks of Pilley's perfect river. She laughs, tells me she thinks my friend and mentor could be feminizing the river a little too directly. "Wife, virgin, mistress, mother," she says. "We've often made the land into a woman in literature." She says it's the baggage we carry around and it shows up often in the speech of outdoor recreationists. She says it's in the way male raft guides often treat and respond to female raft guides. Or especially in how an average boat full of males will respond to a female guide. "What are you doing here?" Lilace says the customers will often be thinking. "You must be a whore, a wild woman or a dyke, or really a man."

"But what about the river, this perfect river?"

Lilace says all rivers are perfect, right? Or at least in the eyes of someone.

I look downstream. I can still see the egret in the distance. It's okay for the egret to spend its day out here on the river hunting, but let Ed Gentry wander off into the woods in his underwear with a bow and arrow and he's automatically privileging masculine aggression.

"If it's not your perfect river," Lilace finally says when I point the egret out to her, "or the perfect river to you, then who are you to tell me it's a better river than the one I might have a stronger bond with?"

I ask Lilace what's wrong with the Chattooga being Pilley's perfect river, and she says, "Nothing." I know that isn't her point. She came to this river with a history and she is realistic about it. It is not an idealized landscape for her, and she doesn't think it should be for anyone. She mentions the raft culture again. "How does the Chattooga enter your life when you're away from the river?" she asks. "How does it shape you even beyond your paddling trips? Those are more interesting questions than whether it's *the* perfect river or not."

The rest of Pilley's birthday trip we chase the egret down the river. The egret keeps its distance, feeding, as we round bend after bend. Often a wading bird will stay just out in front of a trip, repeatedly taking flight and landing nervously a few hundred yards ahead, putting just enough river between its edgy feeding and the strange, brightly colored boats. The bird we trail this afternoon has good hunting in these late summer days. The water is channeled severely and minnows are congregated in the deeper water on the outside of bends. When I'm off the river I'll think of this as metaphor, as prophecy, this hunting in dry times.

The Narrows

SECTION III

FROM

SANDY FORD

TO

FALL CREEK

Because of the intricate, complex
nature of the land, it is not always
possible for a storyteller to grasp
what is contained in a story.
The intent of the storyteller,
then, must be to evoke, honestly,
some single aspect of all that
the land contains.

BARRY LOPEZ

Landscape and Narrative

THE NEXT SPRING I'm back on Section III with Pilley. After
we set the shuttle, we're surprised to see that it's just us this time in
the gravel parking lot at Sandy Ford, two veteran kayakers dressing
out in the chilly Saturday morning air. Before we left Spartanburg I
checked the gauge by phone and found the water's up over two feet.
The level is high and so we expected a good crowd to show up. Maybe
everyone's downstream on Section IV. It doesn't matter. We're just
happy to have stolen a day on this busy April weekend to drive over
and run five miles of the river from Sandy Ford down to Fall Creek.

I'm complaining about the cold. Pilley reminds me that a cold
day on the Chattooga is better than a warm day at a desk or watching a basketball game on TV. I tell him what he's saying sounds like
a bumper sticker.

Pilley, like many guidebooks, calls this run the classic for weekend paddlers out for scenery and adrenaline. One hundred and fifty
yards of bold, continuous ledges and grabby holes of the Class IV
Narrows lie just around a left bend from the put-in. With our boats

on our shoulders we hike down to the edge of the bold river, stretch a little, and slip into our cockpits. Pilley reminds me to offer the kayaker's prayer and I do. "Protect us from sneakers, and keepers, and old spray skirts leaking, and things that go bump on my boat," I intone. Pilley's always liked the way my literary mind works over things and finds ways to add ritual and romance to our river trips. "You see much more than what is there," he often says, laughing when I start into one of my explanations of landscape or culture. "You poets see a much bigger world wherever you look."

Of course, I think of the poet and novelist James Dickey and how big a world he saw. He was maybe the master of the imagination. One friend who knew Dickey at USC said once, when I asked about the "lies" that Dickey's biographer Henry Hart made the focus of the poet's life, "Other people took Jim literally, but he himself lived in a totally figurative world." I know the dance between truth and the imagination is an important one. I just don't know who is supposed to lead. I think this is something I probably share with James Dickey, and I point it out to Pilley.

Pilley, a scientist, isn't surprised. He's more amused. He believes fact should lead our steps into understanding, though the way the world gets bigger through a poet's eyes intrigues him enough to continue the conversation.

The Narrows, where we are now headed, is hugely significant for me, much bigger than life and the facts of the rapid, even bigger than the memories I have from running it a few dozen times. Approaching the rapid and accompanying gorge has always summoned paddling's demons. I think it's the story Pilley once told me of floating up on the body of a dead paddler, a canoeist, in the winter of '72 or '73. Pilley can't remember the exact year. It was back before the Forest Service began to regulate use, and Pilley used to drive over from Wofford on Saturday mornings like this one, carry his Grumman canoe the quarter mile down to Sandy Ford, float down to the take-out by himself, and then, after the run, hitchhike back to where he started to pick up his car.

This solitary experience that's so much a part of Pilley's memory as a Chattooga pioneer is illegal today. We are at the minimum of legality—two boats—for a floating party's safety established and regulated by the Forest Service.

So much of the Chattooga lives in stories. Many of those stories are about the early days of white water, when the river was more mysterious, less understood, and less regulated. And more dangerous, if the number of drownings in the early years is any indication. All my trips down the river make up some percentage of the cultural life of the stream, but much of that culture survives in what others have told me. Pilley's stories are some of the first I remember.

I'm not suggesting that John Pilley is in some way at the center of the story of this river. It's more that Pilley's is the channel through which so much of the river's lore has passed to me. Others had more essential roles as explorers and advocates for the river's protection: Frank Bell Jr. and Frank Bell Sr., Hugh Caldwell, Fritz Orr Jr., Romone Eaten, Bunny Johns, Jimmy Holcombe, Randy Carter, Jay Evans, John Burton, Claude Terry, Payson Kennedy, Horace Holden Sr., Jim Griner, Doug Woodward, Herb Barks, and Tommy Wyche, to name only a few. These paddling pioneers from the fifties, sixties, and seventies will be associated—through story and lore—with this Wild and Scenic River forever.

From the beginning of this descent of the Chattooga I've wondered how I will give all those whose lives crossed paths with the river their due. I know now, over halfway down, it's impossible. In long conversations with early paddlers like Payson and Aurelia Kennedy, two of the Nantahala Outdoor Center's founders, I've always returned to the origin stories, the tales of the discovery runs in the 1960s. Often they are more interesting than the story Dickey made up. The Kennedys' story is typical of many I've heard.

Payson and Aurelia paddled the Chattooga for the first time in 1965, soon after they had returned to Atlanta after a decade away. Payson and Relia had done some camp paddling as kids in the mountains of north Georgia and a little as adults. In 1965, Payson was working as a librarian at Georgia Tech. Relia was teaching elementary school.

They had heard about the Chattooga from Atlanta friend Horace Holden, who had heard about it from "camp friends." So in October the Holdens and the Kennedys, with six children in tow, went up into north Georgia to give this new river a try.

They'd only looked at a highway map. Holden had some directions on a piece of paper, but they blew out the window on the way up.

The first morning, they split into two groups. One group, Horace, Payson, and Relia, went in one tandem and one solo canoe. Jody, Horace's wife, took the van and the kids and planned to meet them downstream at Earl's Ford. In the two Grummans, the first group floated from Pine Mountain, on the West Fork, down to Turn Hole Rapids, about three miles above Earl's Ford, where they all camped for the night. Next morning, Jody switched with Relia, and they continued downstream. Relia followed in the van with the kids. The plan was for her to pick everyone up late in the afternoon at the Highway 76 bridge.

By 3 P.M. Payson and Horace figured they weren't far from the Highway 76 bridge. It was only in retrospect that they realized how wrong they were.

"We weren't strong paddlers and we all found some of the rapids hard to scout," Payson explained when I talked with the Kennedys at their house on the Nantahala River over three decades later. They portaged some rapids. Some they stood and studied a long time before running. Payson remembers that one they studied was what would later be known as Second Ledge, which back then looked a lot worse than it is now.

By the time it was dark, they were only through what is now Eye-of-the-Needle, still six miles above Highway 76. They ran some of that stretch of the river—including a rapid called Roller Coaster—in the dark. They decided to stop for the night, not knowing what was below. Payson had matches in a bamboo match case and some extra clothes. They lay by the fire all night. First light, they went downstream and found they were above Painted Rock, the Class IV known in the early days as Keyhole. When they reached Bull Sluice, they portaged that Class V and made contact with a search party headed upstream.

Later they learned that Relia had waited at the highway crossing until dark and then walked upstream and seen Bull Sluice. "I knew all the paddlers had good sense and would hear the rapids," she said. "I was calm and I had a lot of faith in their ability." Still, she went to the sheriff's office and told them they were missing on the river when they did not show up. The search party assumed they were hurt, and Relia took the kids back to Atlanta that night. She actually went to school and taught the next day, not knowing the fate of the Chattooga adventurers.

Horace Holden's father was a judge and he actually had the National Guard called out to search for the lost paddlers. "We were embarrassed," Payson said. "We were okay and never in any danger."

After that first trip, the river was in everybody's blood. Next summer, they all came back to run Section IV. By 1971, Payson's knowledge of the Chattooga and skill with a canoe earned him a spot, with Claude Terry and Doug Woodward, as a paddling double during the filming of *Deliverance*. That year, Payson and Relia left Atlanta to found, with the Holdens, the Nantahala Outdoor Center in Wesser, North Carolina. In 1972, the NOC began to run raft trips out of outposts in the Chattooga watershed. After 1974, when the river was granted Wild and Scenic River status, NOC, along with Wildwater and Southeastern, was granted a permit to conduct raft trips on the river. In less than ten years, Payson saw his own adventurous trip on a white-water river transformed into a business that today has given hundreds of thousands the chance to float the river.

"I like the stories," John Pilley says. "You know, where the river comes along with the people." We've been floating at a steady pace, and most of the last mile I've been telling Pilley about Payson Kennedy's first trip down the river. Pilley says he didn't know Payson in those early years, but that story sounded like lots of others he'd heard. "It was all a big adventure back then."

Soon as the Narrows comes into view, the river changes moods, gets all stirred up, drops over three ledges before constricting and disappearing into a brief, dark gorge. The sound of roaring water echoes off the shadowy walls. Hemlocks lean in for the diminishing light. I follow Pilley into the rapid on river left, and we work down over and through the three ledges, looking for clear black tongues of water between the hydraulics. The current flushes through, even when the river is at lower levels. After this long entrance we are in the gorge proper, and the water swirls, eddies, piles up on itself. There are few places to stop our boats and sit comfortably in the chaos. Beginners fear this crazy water more than the difficulty of traversing the ledges above. There's something deeply frightening about water that has no surface logic, going in many directions at once. After a peel-out into the current, we take two more ledges, following as the river narrows even more and flows between vertical cliffs and huge black boulders, and end up in an eddy at the bottom.

As we sit in the eddy, Pilley remembers how he floated up on the body at the exit to this brief gorge, just past us, where the river widens again. As we sit in the eddy and look back upstream into the dark reaches of the Narrows, Pilley tells me the man's body was snagged on a hemlock. He didn't linger after he'd spotted it. Pilley was committed to the river and would report the victim when he got downstream to the Highway 76 bridge take-out twelve miles below. There was nothing he could do. The paddler was dead. After Pilley ran Second Ledge, a drop that is usually fun, a straightforward run down into a large pool, Pilley floated up on people downstream looking for the body. He told them it was upstream, and they all headed up the bank to recover it.

There were eighteen deaths on the Chattooga between 1970 and 1978, so a search for a dead body was not uncommon in those early years. Often as not, the victims were people with no experience with rivers, inner-tubers, or drunk men in army surplus rafts prepared by ignorance to duplicate the *Deliverance* story. Most of the boaters who died in the rapids launched into the current uncertain of their fate, with no skill, no sense of the danger always ahead on the Chattooga. As late as 1990 an eleven-year-old child drowned in the Narrows. His kayak had overturned and his foot was entrapped as he swam through the ledges. The place has always been dark. There will be others, some experienced, others with no understanding of the shadowy logic a white-water river works with the unsuspecting.

I've run this section of the river many times, but of all the Chattooga's watery landscapes, this is the one that I dream about. Nothing bad has ever happened to me in the Narrows, but the topography of the stretch can etch deep lines in your memory.

The brief stretch of river around the Narrows is essential gorge country, the kind of psychological landscape Dickey builds the plot of *Deliverance* around. In order for his mythic story to work, Dickey had to get his characters to drop deeper and deeper into the earth, the very bowels of the country. They had to get down and away from any form of civilization. A river on its way to the ocean cuts through stone and lays open such topography. A cave (which Walker Percy uses in one of his later southern novels) is another landscape available for such encounters with our darkest nemesis: death.

Even on a day like this one—uncommon, easy, relaxing, and approaching warmth as the sun finally rock hops over the ridges sheltering the river—the thought of the "river as death" is never far from me. This darkness stays on my mind until we pass fully out of the Narrows with its concrete symbolism of dark vertical space compromised by destructive water and bad luck or poor decisions.

The Narrows is the only place on Section III or IV of the Chattooga that matches what one of the gas station attendants says to Drew near the beginning of *Deliverance:* down in that gorge, he explains, "The water climbs them rock walls like a monkey." Looking back upstream I can see the monkeys playing along the base of the cliffs. Not real monkeys, as Pilley would point out, but others, the monkeys of imagination and adventure.

I know from memory of other trips that below the Narrows the river widens and the surrounding terrain flattens out some. After a quarter mile the horizon line announces Second Ledge, a six-foot vertical ledge that is best run on the far left, just a few yards from the South Carolina side. I remember Lee Hagglund's story of Pilley leading him over Second Ledge without warning as I eddy behind a rock upstream of the drop and peel out and line up the bow of my kayak. I smile as I power ahead and slip over the drop. In a split second I'm safe in the eddy below.

The first time I ran Second Ledge it felt like Niagara Falls or the waterfall the adventurers in *Deliverance* spill over. After twenty or thirty times (or in Pilley's case, countless) the drop is more like cresting the top of a hill in a roller coaster and throwing up your hands as the bottom falls out.

We stop there, on a beach jutting off the Georgia side. It's the kind of place you fall in love with on the Chattooga, a gathering spot with a good river-wide surfing wave that gets better and better as the water rises.

Below Second Ledge the river settles down and the scenery, as always, is spectacular—hemlock groves, the first of the redbud blooming, and huge rocks lining the riversides. The lavender redbud is called Judas tree, since it usually shows its color near Easter. In the dark spring woods, it stands out along the river's edges, reaching into the light.

Dickey loved Christian metaphors like resurrection and deliverance, and he loved the metaphor of drowning. It's in a gorge like we've just passed through that Dickey has Drew meet his final fate, possibly shot from above, possibly drowned when he falls out of the bow of Ed's canoe. It's also where Ed survives and begins his transformation to savior of Lewis and Bobby. It is in this landscape of ledges and rapids that I think I was delivered—from what, I can never be sure. What waited downstream for me had my life not crossed the course of this river?

Downstream we cruise through Eye-of-the-Needle—Pilley leading and remembering his way through this fast, constricted, Class III chute along the left bank. Pilley follows the glassy tongue of water down the left, traveling fast with the current, and then places a sea-soned draw stroke in on the right and slips past the large boulder where many novice paddlers have ended up on their first trip through "the eye."

Pilley's application of a draw stroke in heavy current is the sort of response that defines a good paddler. They say poetry is the right words in the right order, and the same can be said for the art of paddling. The poetry of white-water paddling is the exact right stroke at the exact right moment, and I'm always impressed by Pilley's fluid technique. He's paddled so many rivers the strokes have become as unconscious as driving a car.

Rivers like the Chattooga demand such control. Even a Class III like Eye-of-the-Needle is unforgiving once you enter it. Good technique determines your fate.

The Eskimo roll, something I haven't used on this spring paddle, is one of the keys to good kayaking technique. It's the way a paddler rights the kayak once it's been tipped over, a graceful acrobatic move that rotates the boat and its occupant out of the dark 180 degrees into the light. If an unprepared novice with a missing or a weak Eskimo roll flips in a kayak in white water, it can be a frightening moment. Often the rapid's channel is shallow, constricted, and fast, and the paddler, tucked up against the bottom of a flipped kayak, has to endure rocks, current, and chaos. The experienced boater with a good roll somehow holds the chaos at bay, no matter how dire the circumstances. It's like constructing a tiny safe womb around you while you set up your paddle and right yourself.

I've rolled on the top of a small waterfall, a place where coming out of the inverted boat would have been quite dangerous. The metaphoric potential for the roll is endless. Righting yourself is a powerful idea when it looks like everything is lost. Popping back up onto the surface of a white-water river looks like some small form of resurrection I'm sure to those who think that it's magic to see the paddler reappear from below the surface.

Below Eye-of-the-Needle there are two more miles of small ledges and fast current. It's another place to simply float and remember all the chaos behind us. Isn't that what paddling white water is about, really? It's the memory of the rapid—and the stories we tell of running it—as much as the rapid itself.

"Let's get on down," Pilley says when he sees me staring back up past Second Ledge toward the Narrows. "Lunch is waiting for us on a rock in the sun somewhere downstream."

Approaching the Bull

SECTION III

FROM

FALL CREEK

TO

SECTION IV

AT

WOODALL SHOALS

These games, these contests,

these grunting conversations

of body to body, father to son,

are not substitutes for other ways

of being alive. They are the

sweat and sweaty thing itself.

SCOTT RUSSELL SANDERS

Hunting for Hope

SIMPLY WANT to get back on the river, but it's taken us longer to find the Fall Creek put-in than we expected. Driving in off Highway 76 we stopped at Bruce Hare's Chattooga Whitewater Shop to ask directions. The shop sits on a hill and is a landmark—a place to stop and confirm a river level, buy a missing piece of equipment or a new boat, or, like us, ask directions. After directions, we somehow miss our turn anyway. I'm driving. I'm talking too much and not watching the road enough. Dykes Blackmon is my copilot. He's a former student of mine, and we have five years to catch up on. When I realize we're lost, I ask Dykes to glance down at his feet and grab the dry bag with the river guidebook in it. "What's the number of that Forest Service road?" He opens the book on his lap, and clarifies, "Stay on Forest Service Road 722."

Rob, my soon-to-be stepson, is pushed in behind the seat with all the gear. He just wants to get to the river. He's fifteen and his frame is already over six feet. Riding all morning in the back of a truck twisted in like some contortionist is not his idea of fun. He shifts from side to side. He listens as we haggle over road numbers and distances.

According to the tiny, green square government road signs with numbers on them, we are on 722, but instead of depositing us at the trailhead above the Chattooga, the gravel road dead-ends in a front yard among a spray of panicked chickens. Briefly I pause in the driveway and take in several abandoned vehicles up on blocks and the tumbledown house wedged between big hemlocks at the end of the drive.

"Where you going, city boy?" I say as I quickly put my old Toyota truck in reverse, mimicking one of the Griner brothers taunting lost Lewis Medlock in *Deliverance*. "It ain't but the goddamn biggest river in the state."

As we drive on through Forest Service land I conclude we should have stayed with the certainty of old pleasures. A river-running creature of habit, I'm not used to breaking up the Chattooga in this (for me) new way. I've always preferred the more popular runs on Section III, a trio of choices: the almost-three-mile sprint from Earl's Ford to Sandy Ford, the day-long almost-thirteen-mile leisurely float from Earl's Ford to the 76 bridge, or the ten-mile run from Sandy Ford to the 76 bridge. Each choice has its pleasures. Each has its advantages. Tradition while running rivers is one advantage that is not overrated. I like the idea of getting to know a river in all its moods, and the more descents of a familiar section in a lifetime, the better you know it.

In my mid-forties I began to think often of my lifetime of rivers and develop the concept as I floated down the Chattooga, Lawson's Fork, the Nantahala, the three rivers I will probably always know best. They are all very different rivers and cover the variety available in the southeastern piedmont and mountains. Lawson's Fork is my home river, a piedmont stream running through Spartanburg prone to pollution and crowding from subdivisions and strip malls. In spite of the river's impaired state, Lawson's Fork reveals its beauty to me each time I paddle there. There are six or seven rapids in the stretch I usually paddle, and when I am lucky enough to catch the river after a thunderstorm or in spring rains, several of the rapids can approach the Chattooga in excitement. I worked in the NOC store on the Nantahala, a swift tourist stream on the flank of the Smokies in western North Carolina. For the better part of a decade I paddled it as a daily discipline. I learned to see past the hundred thousand rafters to the river beyond.

I've somehow made it past the twenty-year mark as a paddler, and still the Chattooga stands at the head of my long list of rivers. On any free weekend I first check the gauge to see where the Chattooga stands. I'd paddle much of it at any level short of flood, but to get friends to go with me it has to be at least 1.4 on the computer gauge for these longer excursions upstream of the Highway 76 bridge.

Today, we choose to paddle what Rob tells us the young boaters are now calling Three and a Half, a run that takes in the last three miles of Section III followed by the first two miles of Section IV down to the Woodall Shoals take-out. The advantage of this run is that it cuts down on some of the slower sections between the Narrows, Second Ledge, and Painted Rock. It's all beautiful river, but in a sport more and more defined by adrenaline, this shortened run is hard to argue with Rob about. To him, floating a river has no real advantage. He's in it for the game, for the play.

As for myself, getting the river under me again is what it's all about, feeling its blue-green current take me along in my outdated kayak, drifting effortlessly in the eternal flow bound for the sea. I'm looking forward to spending another spring day spotting some migrating warblers, pondering the endless mystery of the Chattooga's bedrock as reflected in which direction the river meanders as we drift between small and medium-sized shoals. I know that if you look close enough, every mile of the Chattooga is different. I look forward to squandering my paddling life imprinting every mile of its shoreline in my memory, slipping into this river like a sacrament.

A few minutes after our detour, we finally park my truck on the Fall Creek gravel circle where 769 ends in the woods. I can see that we're in the right place. Off to the south, the trail drops a quarter mile through the Wild and Scenic River corridor woods to the river.

Rob unfolds himself from the back of the truck, where he was more cramped than in his impossibly tiny yellow Riot Dominatrix. He yawns and begins to unload his gear. He's already paddled this section of the Chattooga three times and I think would admit up front he's a little bored by the middle-aged pace I set. There's one challenge left for him now, the plum in the middle of the day's harvest of rapids, Bull Sluice, the Class V rapid three miles downstream on Section III.

After a month last summer of camp paddling, Rob can add Class IV rapids on the Chattooga, Ocoee, and Upper Green to his checklist. I tell him that he's only experienced low water, that paddling will change the first time his confidence is shaken and he's throbbed in a grabby hole at high water. He listens, and I must admit that so far he has shown great restraint, walking around Bull Sluice the first three times he's run this section.

Today he will not portage. He's confident, a strong paddler, and he knows the river's not really high enough at 1.6 to complicate things for his youthful vision or honest assessment of his skills. He continues digging his gear out of the back of the truck and piles it on the ground next to his yellow kayak—PFD, spray skirt, new blue dry top (Christmas gift), blue helmet (birthday gift), and a brand-new purchased-yesterday narrow-spouted Nalgene water bottle with a length of orange climbing rope duct-taped to the fat middle.

Rob looks like he's thinking as he inventories his gear a final time. Is he thinking about this glorious river? I'm proud the Chattooga and river running have already gotten into his blood. He knows the rapids and the routes through each difficult passage, though he still tends to let me lead. He's impressed with the river and I think at times even falls victim to its remoteness and beauty. At least that's what I want to think as he floats between rapids on what I think is the most beautiful river in the world.

He announces as I finish unloading my gear from the truck that today's his day. "I'm running Bull Sluice. The double drop," Rob says, then thinks better of it and directs a correction toward me. "Well, I'm running what you run, single or double drop."

We fill out a permit, gear up in the parking lot. Inking in the numbers, I'm thinking about *Deliverance,* the movie. What would Lewis think of this simple process of recording our trip down the river?

I bring up the film and Dykes says he watched ten minutes of it on TBS a few weeks ago. What does this new generation think of the classic struggle of good versus evil as portrayed by John Boorman thirty years ago? Dykes says he's seen *Deliverance* a number of times and Rob's watched it once with me and seemed to enjoy it. Rob's enjoyment had little to do with the movie's complex relationship with this river though. It had more to do with the film as forbidden object. "Most of my friends' parents wouldn't let them watch that movie," he says when I asked him what he thought about it. "Well, what did you think of the river scenes?" I asked, avoiding the issue of the film's violent male-on-male rape. "Canoeing is for old people," he says, smiling, the James Dean of recreational paddling.

Now Rob hauls his boat on down the trail out in front of me and I have to admit he doesn't really fit any of the character profiles of Dickey's four adventurers. He has none of Lewis's discontent with civilization, and he's too young to know Ed's boredom with job and family. Drew's brittle morality hasn't shown its head, and Bobby's lack of awareness and skill outdoors is something he might ridicule in others. He's grown up in a world where river running is a middle-class recreation and most kids play organized sports. He teaches kayaking at camp, and many of the kids in his cabin have already experienced a white-water river on a raft trip. They've already been "deliveranced" by the commercial rafting business.

Walking down, it is Rob's lucky day. A folded five-dollar bill is at his feet in the gravel. "Another Subway foot-long with your name on it," I say as I point it out. He bends down, impossibly tiny yellow boat balanced on his shoulder, and picks it up.

I take Rob in as he straightens up and pushes on down the trail. He's dressed in his blue and yellow Hawaiian shorts just like all the other hair boaters he emulates. He's tall and young and loud and there's so much about him for an aging stepfather kayaker to love.

Outmoded and moldy, I glance down at my frayed dry top and ten-year-old battered creek boat. I always wanted to be a kayker that somebody admired, and I hope to Rob I'm not some old kayaker caught in amber and better off propped up in the lobby of the Perception kayak company. I don't think he's given up on me. Each time we go in an outfitter's shop he points out the playboats he thinks I might fit in, find comfortable. I'll admit that recently I've been pulling them off the shelf and folding my old legs inside. Maybe someday I'll reenter the flow and buy some unbelievably small boat with shovelnose and a flat bottom.

But at least today Rob still needs me. Finally at the river I have to help him pull on the tight high-performance spray skirt. I lean back and pull, pop it on his tiny Riot Dominatrix. He knows the sexist names this outlaw kayak company prefers burn up the seventies liberal in me. Is it only men who buy these boats and paddle them? I think as I snap the skirt tight over the front lip of the cockpit. Lip. Cockpit. Spray skirt. Kayaking has always been shot through with sex, so I keep my prejudices to myself, see no reason to press a philosophical issue on such a bracing morning in the mountains.

We put on at 10 A.M. and head downstream. The water is green and cold. Rocks ripple the surface like turtles. It's not really spring yet at this altitude, but some poplars have begun to leaf out. The dogwoods are still only buds. On the river I notice the numbers of hemlocks as I never have before. There's been a terrible report circulating concerning a pest that could kill all the trees, the hemlock wooly adelgid. This pest probably arrived in the United States from Asia in landscaping trees fifty years ago. The insect infests a tree, attaching itself, and the needles turn color and fall off. Limbs then die, and in less than a decade a whole tree can die.

Reports show the wooly adelgid has been eating the trees from Maine to South Carolina. Some estimates are that the entire east coast range of the trees could be infested in twenty years. In Shenandoah National Park in Virginia only 10 percent of the hemlocks are healthy. "We could lose them all," said a local biologist. Just this week a story in the local paper explained how forestry officials hope releasing imported Japanese beetles will help save the hemlock trees. Though there are many risks to bringing in outside pests, Buzz and the Chattooga Conservancy have endorsed the attempt by the Forest Service to control the wooly adelgid by way of these foreigners. "We're at our wit's end," one of the conservancy's spokespeople said in the paper.

Floating along I keep thinking of all those dead hemlocks. What would we do paddling through such a die-off?

On this first stretch of the river there's some small stuff, mere riffles, and we soon float past Fall Creek Falls, a half mile downstream. The waterfall appears from among the still-healthy hemlocks and mountain laurel, stair-stepping fifteen feet down to the river.

I am happy to be on the river. I finally have sheets of time stretching before me to renew my acquaintance with Dykes. We begin our floating conversation, and he reminds me that it was I who introduced him to white water and the Chattooga. In Dykes's freshman year, 1993, his entire class came to the Chattooga for a weekend. It was a class where we studied nature writers and I had added in a field component, a full-scale canoe clinic required of all the students.

Dykes recalls that our clinic was on a cold November weekend and that we'd stopped to build a fire on a Section III beach to warm up. One girl was close to hypothermia. "College was great," he says remembering the experience now almost a decade in the past. "I called up my parents that week and said, 'Mom and Dad, I'm paddling the Chattooga this weekend for an English class.'"

Back in the days when Dykes was my student most of my best teaching was done from the seat of a kayak. Every weekend I headed out with a group of students to paddle a river somewhere. Sometimes it was wedged into the requirements for a class and sometimes it was time off the clock.

"You're just another one of those students I misdirected by introducing them to white water," I say, laughing, as Dykes explains how it was because of me that he took a kayak clinic at NOC and later ended up almost dead on this very river. "Five years ago, Screaming Left Turn at 2.6," he said. "I swam down there, got knocked silly, and woke up washed onto a beach with one of my Wofford buddies shaking me saying, 'You alive? You alive?'"

Dykes asks about my upcoming wedding as he floats closer beside me and rafts up his kayak with mine. Dykes doesn't say so, but I imagine that back then all my former students saw me as the perennial bachelor, the footloose poet, always headed for a wild river somewhere. I sense in his questions about the wedding, the house, and Betsy that he respects the choices I've made and that these concessions to "normalcy" may actually make his old teacher more human. It's one of the benefits to my changing life that I didn't anticipate.

There must be something appealing to Dykes about settling down. He's in his late twenties, and mentions that he's entered that period where all his college friends are getting married. In Deliverance the issues of normalcy are never far below the surface. What, if not normal life, is Ed hoping for deliverance from? It's wife and job and family and home that he's bored with. It's this bedrock of human culture that Lewis has somehow shed in order to become the hunter, the adventurer who takes the suburbanites down the river. I'm still hopeful that paddling rivers will be part of the warp and weft of my domesticity. After all, our house under construction up the hill from Lawson's Fork has a boat garage in the plans.

One of the key differences between *Deliverance* the novel and *Deliverance* the film is the way each deals with the question of what the adventurers are separating from. The novel sets up the three-day river trip with a section called "Before." In the first twenty pages, Dickey indicates that the characters wish to separate from domesticity and the mundane. Ed, through his first-person narrative, defines his life and the lives of the other three men. Ed wants to have a break from his wife and his work. Bobby is "pleasantly cynical." Lewis's river trip is no different. Drew is the hardest to convince to come along.

"They tell me that this is the kind of thing that gets hold of middle-class householders every once in a while," Ed remembers Bobby saying, "but most of them lie down till the feeling passes."

Lewis suffers from deep boredom with middle-class life. Getting out on the river is a matter of life and death: "And when most of them lie down they're at Woodlawn before they think about getting up."

I'm not certain that we're not better off today. Would Lewis consider our day trip to the Chattooga little better than a visit to the country club? I'll try not to let such speculations on how a fictional character might judge my actions sully my recreation.

It's still cold at 10 A.M. in early April, and we get a wake-up call in a sequence of standing waves called Roller Coaster, the first Class III we've encountered since we put on. I lead, rocking and rolling with the waves to the bottom. I look back over my shoulder. Rob's zipping along. Dykes looks a little shaky. He's getting his boat under him and trying to quiet the Chattooga demons. I imagine what he's thinking. How hard is it to recover a love for floating rivers after what he remembers as a near-death experience? As we floated along upstream, Dykes made me promise I'd watch out for him.

Just past a sharp right-hand bend in the river, Painted Rock looms. It's the first Class IV on the stretch today. There's a scouting beach on the left of this drop, but I decide simply to tell Dykes how to run it and move on ahead. I pull up next to his boat and explain there's a tricky rapid approaching. He's trusting and takes my directions and looks downstream to where a small pulsing wave marks the entry line.

The rapid's name, Painted Rock, suggests the number of canoes that have carried off a frontal assault on an undercut rock that blocks a straight run and deposited a little sample of paint or plastic as a calling card. The drop consists of several ledges with tricky holes that wash down into the round undercut. "Start center and then angle right and try and catch the eddy behind the big rock on river right at the bottom," I tell Dykes before I peel out and start my run.

I catch the eddy behind the big rock and then wait as Rob follows me down. I remember our first descent together of Section III. It had been a low-water run and Painted Rock was Rob's first Class IV rapid. The power of the water had surprised him even at a low flow. This time he has no trouble with it, powering beautifully through the offset hole at the top and on down into the eddy where I wait.

Dykes finds it a little tricky and flips at the top, but he rolls before there's trouble with the undercut. In a moment his Big EZ playboat is bobbing with us in the eddy. I'm relieved to see that he's got a solid roll, and I don't worry that he won't be able to use it today.

It turns into a bird day the next three miles, with kingfishers following us. Once I skirt a big boulder and float up on a single goose roosting on a river rock midcurrent. The bird doesn't hear me coming, but when it finally pulls a brown and black head out from under its wing I float past and it doesn't move. Later we pick up two ospreys circling in the deep gap the trees form above the river. "That's a good sign," Dykes says. "The river's healthy and the fishing's good."

With mild rapids and quiet scenery it's possible on this stretch to float and talk. Along the way Dykes explains to me what he does for a living now five years after a biology degree at Wofford—renovating historic warehouses in his hometown of Columbus for tax credits. He's also a Chattahoochee River Keeper in Columbus and says that they're close to opening a white-water park downtown if they remove two old milldams. "The guy who designed the Ocoee Olympic course has been there twice," he explains. "They've mapped the whole river bottom and they can chart all the rapids."

How strange this will be. Nobody pictures Columbus, Georgia, as a white-water town, but this set of Chattahoochee rapids—a gradient of 120 feet in two miles—is right on the fall line. "After Columbus, nothing but flat water all the way to the Gulf." I like that—the Chattahoochee being set free to snarl and bubble around rocks one final time before it settles down and slides free to the Gulf.

As we float along I ask Dykes if he knows that the Chattooga used to be the headwaters of the Chattahoochee. Before he responds, and I get a chance to finish my lecture in geology, the river sweeps to the left. As we round the bend I can see ahead of us in the distance the river channeling between massive boulders. The nature of the terrain has changed. The sound of roaring water can be heard below the great gray boulders. The sound grabs all our attention.

"I'd like to have seen the water that put them up there," I say as we come around the bend. I point out the big hogback scouting boulder a few hundred yards downstream. We can see two bleached trunks of hemlocks sprawled fifteen feet on top. "Bull Sluice," I say.

The late Sewanee University philosophy professor Hugh Caldwell's first descent of Section III was in the summer of 1952. He worked at Camp Merrie-Woode, a girls' camp five miles from the headwaters of the Chattooga. That summer he was scouting new trips for the campers and saw the Chattooga on a road map. A staff member dropped him off at the Highway 28 bridge at dawn, and he hoped to make the Highway 76 bridge before dark. He had not consulted any topo maps so he had no idea where or if he could get off the river if he needed to. He wasn't even wearing a life jacket (now called a PFD), which was not uncommon among experienced paddlers, at least in the South, in the 1950s.

It rained most of the day and the river rose as Caldwell paddled. He was so uncomfortable that by midafternoon he had ceased scouting rapids because he was uncertain he could make the Highway 76 bridge before dark. He only flipped twice. One of the two flips led to a broach of the eighteen-foot keeled Grumman on what would become known as Keyhole, and then later as Painted Rock. His canoe bent, but it didn't fold, and it took him a long time to free it from the current.

It was nearly dark when Caldwell "blundered" into Bull Sluice. He did not have time to eddy out and so he chose what he thought was the best route, but the drop swamped his canoe and flushed him out. Caldwell didn't notice the Highway 76 bridge just downstream, so, discouraged, he pulled his battered canoe up on what is now the Section IV launching beach on river left. He had not seen a soul since he put in that morning at dawn.

"My long day on the Chattooga left me physically spent," Caldwell said years after the event in a letter to Payson Kennedy. "For days my elbow joints were so sore from drawing the cumbersome 18-foot Grumman that it hurt to raise a glass of water." He says he avoided the Chattooga for a few years, but within a few more "we were running Section 3 with our advanced campers and Section 2 with intermediates."

"The only really safe way to run Bull Sluice is on foot, with your boat on your head," one of the guidebooks for the river still claims. We've left our boats on the upstream beach and rock-hopped to the hogback boulder to eat Power Bars and gaze at the Bull. Rob uncorks his new water bottle, tilts it back. Dykes levers a slab of cheddar cheese off a block I've bought at a convenience store on the trip down. The sun is layered behind a slab of thick cloud. It's cold. From this safe distance I can see the monster current (even at 1.6) moving over the rocks below me.

I stand and look at the Bull. Just below us, on the Georgia side, a veteran river guide walks what seems two novice outfitter trainees to the edge of the trough paddlers call the double drop. I've seen this guide before, though I can't remember which of the three companies he works with. He has Hawaiian shorts just like Rob's. He's barefooted in the cold and strokes his long billy goat goatee as he talks and looks at the river. There's something dramatic about him. Maybe it's the fact his head is topped with a fiberglass helmet with painted horns that looks like a prop from a Wagner opera.

The two novices watch intently. The raft-guide Yoda in the sparkly Viking helmet tosses a pebble toward a round, dark depression on the shelf above the drop—one of the prominent and infamous features of the Bull. Water rushes over the oval sinkhole, and one tiny pressure wave kicks into the air near where the river guide's pebble hits.

"This is the famous suck hole," he tells the two novices, "where several swimmers have died over the years."

"And this," he says as he tosses another pebble, "is Decapitation Rock." As the guide talks, I point out for Dykes the huge slab of stone sticking like a nose in the middle of the river-wide ledge. Today it is visible in the rushing current. A third of the current flows out of the eddy and straight over the ledge extending to the South Carolina side, and two-thirds of the current flows directly into the trough that forms the double drop on the Georgia side. I describe for him how Decap, as everyone calls it, creates the downstream dividing line between the two classic runs of Bull Sluice.

The easier run, called single drop, is a simple peel-out and then descent straight over the sloping slide to the left of Decap. The trickier run is the double drop. In this one you ferry upstream against the current and point for the Georgia side and paddle over the ledge and brace into a ninety-degree trough that drains its frothing chaos back into the river over the second drop just to the Georgia side of Decapitation Rock.

Dykes looks a little worried as he stares at this stretch of water he has not visited in over four years. He looks down at the Bull and says he's decided he's not going to run it today. He'll walk his boat around. I agree, though I know he might have a little trouble making the big South Carolina–side eddy above the drops. I suggest that he paddle down into the eddy and then walk his boat down from there. I remind him it's a much easier portage from there than the Georgia side. "From over here, it's a Class V rapid, and Class IV portage," I joke.

Dykes thinks about it, says, "What the hell," that he's already had to roll once today, at Painted Rock. He says he'll take my advice and follow us into the big eddy on river left. If you don't want to run something, it's always best to put your boat on your shoulder and carry it around a rapid, but the choice is always that of the paddler.

I turn back to the instruction in progress below. I envy the guide's patience, how he turns our waterfall into a classroom for new guides. I have no such skill. This stretch of white water makes my stomach do flip-flops. Maybe it's the ten people who have died here. Maybe it's something deeper than death. But what's deeper than death? Many of the deaths here have been because of ignorance. Six died here in the 1970s, beginning soon after *Deliverance* was filmed. In that wild decade victims floated through from overturned rafts, canoes, and inner-tubes, all like Caldwell, not wearing a life jackets in those days before it was required by the Forest Service. In the 1980s the victims included people with more white-water experience: one man, a guide for an outfitting company, stepped out of his canoe at the top of the ledge to free his boat, caught his leg in the pothole, and drowned when the current forced him under. The same year, a woman bodysurfing was caught between the hydraulic and Decapitation Rock and drowned when her friends could not free her. In the mid-1990s a man was swimming below the Bull without a PFD and nearly drowned in the current. He was rescued and EMS was called. In 1997, when the last death occurred, a seasonal farmworker who could not speak English drowned while swimming below Bull Sluice.

I look upstream and try to focus on the slower water up near where boats beach for scouting on the Georgia side. Every inch of water between here and there is on a greased slide around each end of the approach rock in midcurrent. I try to think about a positive run. I keep seeing my kayak breaking through the approach waves and sliding safely into the eddy above the big drops.

Looking down at the Bull, I'm lost in all the chaos. I keep hearing Terry's "bowling alley" in the Bull's relatively low flow. What's bedrock and what's boulder? The white water we see gone lacy in river calenders is really just bubbles rising off the river's labor. The language of this rapid is one of power, scour, and grind. Nothing loves down like a river. Bedrock is where a mountain stream wants to sleep and dirty the sheets with boulders, cobbles, pebbles, gravel, sand, silt, and clay. Look in these spots and you'll see nature's cost accounting a thousand years hence.

After too much reflection time, the three of us pick up our helmets and walk through the stream-rounded boulders back to our boats beached above the drop. We pull on our spray skirts and work out into the current. I'm leading, with Rob right behind, followed by Dykes. As I head down through the fast water and waves that guard the eddy above the drops, I realize I'm a little too far right and fight hard into the eddy, spinning in the slack water behind the jutting rocks from the South Carolina side. I'm a little worried that I've led Rob too far right and he will not be able to make the eddy turn, but soon my fears diminish as I see that Rob is fine. He's focused and aware on this first run of Bull Sluice. In a split second, his yellow Riot sits beside me in the eddy. "That wasn't so hard," he says as he rests in the eddy. I look back over my shoulder and can see the small wave popping up that marks the spot I plan to hit for the single drop. I point it out to Rob and tell him to follow me there when we finally run the rapid soon as Dykes is safely in the eddy and has his short portage in progress.

Paddling hard a few dozen yards behind Rob, Dykes is even further right than we had been. I'm worried he's going to completely miss the safe eddy I've directed him to and continue through the rapid over the double drop. Soon as he hits the approach waves guarding the eddy, the unfolding scenario gets worse: Dykes flips in the standing waves and soon passes us upside down a dozen fast yards from the drop. All Rob and I can see from the eddy is the yellow plastic bottom of Dykes's kayak amid the bubbly water flowing over the ledge.

I look for his paddle to see if he's setting up. "Roll," I say. "Roll that boat, Dykes." The last thing I want to see is my former student out of his boat swimming over Bull Sluice. I also don't want him upside down in his boat as he tumbles into the sticky hydraulic at the base of the trough that forms half of the infamous double drop.

I want to see him upright and heading downstream, even if he rolls on the lip of the drop itself.

A split second later Dykes is up, his head and torso bobbing upright. He's too late to catch the eddy though, and as soon as we see he's up he disappears over the horizon line of the double drop and out of sight downstream. I peel out, leaving Rob sitting safely in the eddy, and disappear over the single drop, hoping I'll see Dykes safe in the big recovery eddy below the Bull.

The single drop is about a six-foot slide, and there's enough water so that I hit the bottom and disappear into a foamy backwash and bob up. When I hit I see that Dykes has somehow survived, in his boat, and is sitting in an eddy river right waiting for us. He looks a little shell-shocked after his unplanned run of the Bull. I look back over my shoulder just in time to see Rob's first run of Bull Sluice, a perfect run down the single drop a little left of where I have hit.

"That was ugly," I say, joking with Dykes sitting safe in the eddy. He smiles, but he's still a little too stunned to converse. "That was one ugly run."

"Class V paddler," I say as Rob plants several strokes, parks his boat beside me in the eddy.

"That wasn't hard," Rob says. "I'm never running the single drop again!"

Below Bull Sluice and around the bend the old steel-beamed Highway 76 bridge looms high above the current. We look up at its rusty brown skeleton from another age. Just beyond us, the newer concrete bridge ferries steady streams of traffic to South Carolina and Georgia.

We pass the Section IV put-in beach on river left where Hugh Caldwell ended his epic journey and now two families sit in lounge chairs in the sand, watching us and the river flow. There are at least three generations playing on the edge of the water, skipping stones, sitting, talking. These visitors are not paddlers, but are part of another brother- and sisterhood of the wild, those who like to sit on a

Sunday in the presence of raw, unharnessed nature and fish or just watch. Their intimacy with and commitment to this river are admirable. I guess they might call it love. They've returned to this place with the regularity of migration, in spite of all the outsiders crowding them since the 1970s. In the old days, before the white-water business, this deep pool and accessible beach below Bull Sluice acted like a community center—fishing, picnicking, even baptism.

We flow on, our destination Woodall Shoals, about two miles downstream where we'll bring this trip to a close. Surfing Rapid, Rob's other highlight for Three and a Half, is just around the next bend. We pass the gauge on the South Carolina side and see that the river's dropped a little since we put on. It sits barely at 1.5. A good level for Section IV. There's nothing predictable about a wild, free-flowing river like the Chattooga. It's not like having a dam upstream adjusting the flow. The levels can go up or down while you're on it. It can rise or drop a foot with summer storms. It's one of the aspects that makes it my favorite river, the difficulty of predicting things.

The subject of predictability reminds me of Rob's love of playboating, the new rage in kayaking and his future. Many of the new young paddlers are "park and play" addicts who drive to well-known waves and friendly hydraulics on accessible rivers and practice their "rodeo" moves over and over. More bronco rider than old-time river runner, the new breed of kayaker paddles short, cramped boats, with scooped-out bows and sterns. Floating is merely a means to an end, the end being play. As a playboater proceeds down a river, below-the-surface currents catch and spin him endlessly. Rather than avoiding them, a playboater sees rocks as props for stunts the way skateboarders use railings and steps, as ways to make the trip more interesting. To toss the boat around in the current wherever it may dwell is the "throw-down" and to move the boat around on a wave is to "shred."

When I started paddling in the 1970s all kayaks were thirteen feet long. Today, most are less than seven feet. The boat bottoms were mostly round in the old days, a way of assuring easy turns and stability. Today the bottoms are mostly flat and allow for spinning ceaselessly on a wave. There are hard edges that paddlers can catch in current. I glance over at Rob's craft, an impressive angular playboat, and marvel at how far things have come in three decades. Rob loves to play and shred as much as I love to float and paddle. I'm not sure I can ever break into the new scene, and I worry I will miss so much of what he loves.

This floating versus playing is a serious generational issue in kayaking, and I mull its elements. Rob approaches kayaking with a base knowledge of skiing, power boating, and even a little skateboarding. I came to white-water boating in 1977 partially as transportation, as a way of getting closer to nature and wild land. When I learned to paddle, I mastered a few strokes and a roll. I learned how to read a river, how to ferry, eddy out, surf, and maybe fire my boat straight in the air out of a hydraulic (an ender). This basic bag of tricks was enough to get me down most rivers (which was my goal) and provided a little fun at a few selected spots along the way. After I'd learned the basics, a river quickly became a path to adventure, maybe even enlightenment.

What I'm talking about is the issue of sport versus recreation. Rob's into kayaking as a sport, *his* sport, the one he has more potential in than soccer, baseball, and basketball. Kayaking today for the young (and the mature boaters who have embraced change) is a sport solidly grounded in motor skills, technique, and expensive designer equipment. The section of the Chattooga we've just left behind is mythic to me. It is a landscape as real and legendary in my mind as a great novel or poem or song. It's something I love and return to with regularity, but I'm afraid that as Rob ages and his skill grows, it will simply become boring and uninteresting to him. Section III is definitely not one of the premier stops on the adrenaline-sports express. What we've just paddled offers no perfect "play holes" and little real challenge for the new experts unless the water starts climbing the gorge walls like a monkey, as the Griner brothers described high water situations to Lewis in *Deliverance.*

Bull Sluice is really the only feature on Section III that catches the attention of many of the new paddlers, the only place with enough staying power to remain legendary in an age when the best paddlers are running thirty-foot waterfalls.

Surfing Rapid offers a common ground for the two of us though. It's one of the classic playspots in the southeast—hence its name. Since the early days with Grumman canoes and self-molded fiberglass kayaks, three generations of boaters have paused here to stick their bows and sterns in the friendly reversing hydraulic and squirrelly eddy known as Surfer's. There's a nice tongue of current to ride down through the rapid, a Class III, and a spot to rest at the bottom. I slide down the tongue and eddy behind the big rock on river right. I think about how many times I've slipped through this slot and sat watching my friends firing off ender after ender in the old long boats. Rob follows me through and stays in the hole surfing a few seconds then draws his bow around and pulls off a piddly little pop-up in his Riot, rights himself with a brace when he lands, then fights the swirling eddy water until he comes to rest next to me and the rock. We watch together as Dykes follows us down and into the eddy.

An ender used to be the ultimate play move using big boats in the old days. We knew where all the ender holes were on all the familiar rivers. This was one of the best. To pop an ender, the paddler surfed a wave upstream until the bow of the boat slid under the falling current and the boat was fired into the air by the power of the water. A good paddler could clear the water, go vertical, and smile at the camera of a buddy in the eddy. It was an impressive sight in a thirteen-foot boat.

Sitting beside me Rob admits that my old, long Perception Overflow is an ideal boat for playing at Surfing Rapid. He says someday he wants to paddle it down and play for two or three hours here. I laugh at the idea and then realize this Chattooga rapid's like one of those old fifties drive-ins with curb service. I tell Rob that maybe someday there will be a retro day on the Chattooga, and everyone will retrieve outdated kayaks from their garages and paddle them down to Surfing Rapid and hold an old-time ender's contest and a twenty-five-years-out-of-production Perception Mirage will win.

"Fat chance," Rob replies.

I watch as he paddles one more time into the current and spins in the Surfing Rapid hole. I'm anticipating the rest of our float and am eager to get on downstream. I'm a little chilly and want to be off the river soon. I peel into the river and pick my way through the rock garden that guards the entrance to Screaming Left Turn.

This is Dykes's dragon rapid. He nearly died here the last time he was on this river, so I take some time to hang back and wait for him. I want to lead him through. Rob paddles ahead of me, remembering Screaming Left Turn as "no big deal" from the other time he's paddled it. At this water level, he's right. It's not a difficult rapid, but I know it's still tricky and I know we have to get Dykes past the Screaming Left Turn memory he carries in his head, the ghost of a bad run. As a very skilled, though still beginning paddler, Rob doesn't have any bad runs yet to remember. For him, so far, there are no paddling ghosts—literal or figurative. There are no hairy swims, no dead friends. In my thirty years of paddling I've lost one close friend and seen one other badly hurt on a river. This historic reality is always with me as I paddle, no matter how good I feel on a river. No one has ever died at Screaming Left Turn, but I know thirty people have died at various places all along this river, some quite surprising. I try to respect the power of the water and hope that Rob does the same. I know Dykes does.

We stop in an eddy just above the rapid and I tell Dykes that the current wants to push a boat into a slab of undercut rock directly in front of the approach. "Remember to take a hard draw and slip left," I say. "Hence the screaming left turn." Dykes remembers the rapid well, but is ready to run it again. I slip through first, drawing my boat to the left, and I eddy at the bottom of the rapid. Dykes runs it perfectly. The roar of the water is refreshing and blocks out all other thoughts. Dykes follows as I peel out and head downstream over several more ledges at the bottom of the rapid.

Soon as the river eases off a little, I look downstream and don't see Rob's boat. He's taken off ahead of us and at first I panic a little, like a father whose small child has wandered off in a crowd. Then I think there's nothing that can hurt him until Woodall Shoals. In spite of it all though, I take off paddling in high gear until I finally see him again at the next Class IV rapid, Rock Jumble. He's waiting for us there. We regroup in the eddy and I don't say anything about my panic, just smile and say, "This is Rock Jumble," and slip down through the boulders into the eddy below.

Rock Jumble is a steep, quick drop of maybe six feet over five yards, a badly broken ledge with no clear tongue of water to ride to the bottom. It's such a shallow place, you don't want to roll there. Rob follows my route left of center and lands easily in the eddy. Dykes has a little more trouble but stays upright through five yards of boulders and current.

A half mile below Rock Jumble we can hear Woodall Shoals, a Class IV rapid with one huge Class VI hydraulic that has claimed eight victims since 1970. The infamous hole at Woodall is to the right of a long rock ledge that we can see extending to the river's center. It's below the horizon line, just past the ledge. I proceed to far river right where there is a shallow slide down into a pool, a sneak route around the hole. At lower water levels skilled boaters run the hole at Woodall, but my old instincts say to stay away from this dragon.

After we traverse the ledges at the bottom of Woodall Shoals, Rob ditches his boat on the cobble beach on river left and cools his cramped feet in the current. I hit the beach as well, climb out, watch as he climbs back in the current, holds a big rock close to his stomach, and attempts to pull off a "mystery move" and travel unseen underwater until he reappears downstream in the big eddy below Woodall Shoals. Maybe the slower sections of the river are a toll the youthful are willing to pay to reach the challenge. Maybe if they had their choice even the Chattooga would morph into one of those challenge-a-minute Six Flags rides. But maybe not. I get the feeling at moments on the river that Rob sees it, the beauty and isolation of this place. Sometimes when he doesn't notice me looking, I catch him just looking around, taking in the vastness of it all. Surely he senses the common good of such experiences. He's a smart fifteen year old. I don't think he would want the Chattooga to be anything different from what it is. I just have to trust him, and trust that strange desire he has for me to be "up-to-date" more than I am. Maybe when I'm John Pilley's age, and Rob's a little younger than I am now, we'll paddle this river together a few more times.

Rob disappears for a moment and then pops up downstream. It's a trick that he learned from his camp instructor the summer before when they finished their Adventure Trek week of rivers here on this beach. I lean back on my boat and consider the Chattooga. It's so many things to so many people. Rob's having a good time. From the look on his face when he surfaces, I can see the long day's paddle was definitely worth it. He'll sleep all the way home. And he'll be back to carry on the tradition.

The Business of White Water

SECTION IV

FROM

HIGHWAY 76

TO

LAKE TUGALOO

Deliverance is not a novel

or a movie anymore.

It's an industry.

JAMES DICKEY

Greenville News, 1980

Y STUDENTS are sleepy and disoriented. It's a chilly October
morning in the South Carolina mountains, and there's even a little
mist over the wetland beside the Nantahala Outdoor Center outpost. The North Face fleeces used as pillows on the ride down are
quickly pulled on. They all look around as if they've landed on Mars.
We've been driving for several hours; and even though I've briefed
them in class the day before as to where the Chattooga is located, to
them, the trip must feel like a foray into how Horace Kephart described the Smoky Mountains over one hundred years ago, the "back
of beyond."

The NOC outpost is thirty miles from the nearest interstate and
nearly that far from anything you could consider a town. We've been
studying water all semester in a paired humanities/biology class—
its physical reality and mythical and metaphorical significance—
and the Chattooga serves today as our example of wild water. NOC
is our transportation into the river corridor below the Highway 76
bridge.

In our class, I've downplayed the Dickey angle, though over half of the students have seen the movie and already refer to the Chattooga as the *Deliverance* river. The sections I've read them from the novel have little to do with the story's violence, even though the famous rape scene and many of the late scenes in the movie were filmed on this stretch of river. Instead I've chosen several scenes where Dickey describes the wildness of a mountain river.

I can see some fear in the eyes of at least one of my students. Tiffany can't swim. She's been fretting for weeks about this trip, though we have trussed her up in a bulky PFD on two occasions already in boats and she's done fine. The Chattooga is something different though—mythic and wild.

Wildness is my academic peg to hang our discussions on for this week. As concept, creed, and experience, wildness interests me, and in turn I try to get my students interested in it as well. In an assignment they've just completed I ask them to consider how writer and activist Rick Bass defines wildness in "River People," an essay in which he floats down the Chattooga and Nantahala Rivers. I'm hoping they will reflect a little deeper as they paddle the very river where he works through his ideas about "wild" and "free." Will this college field experience offer more than a Six Flags ride? We're now, as Cat Stevens said in the 1970s, on the way to find out.

At the check-in desk, the trip leader confirms that I've sent in over one thousand dollars to the Nantahala Outdoor Center, payment in full to take fifteen students, two preceptors, and three Wofford faculty on a raft trip down Section IV of the Chattooga. It's early October, the end of the season. Rates are higher in the summer, so we've been given the off-season discount, plus the institutional rate reduction. Two months earlier, I'd called the number for reservations at the main NOC outpost, in Wesser, North Carolina, on the Nantahala River. There, in a two-story gray shingle house the reservation staff schedules raft trips on five different rivers—the Ocoee, French Broad, Nantahala, Nolichucky, and Chattooga—plus they sign up participants in canoe, kayak, mountain bike, and climbing clinics. There are also always a few overseas "adventure travel" trips to book as well. I could have shopped around and maybe gotten a slightly lower rate with one of the two competing raft companies on the Chattooga—Wildwater or Southeastern—but NOC is my former employer and I feel a certain kinship and loyalty. I know it's a good value. NOC is known as the Harvard of outdoor recreation.

By 8:30 A.M. we're checked in and watching the safety video in the gear barn surrounded by PFDs, wet suits, splash tops, and helmets. It looks like the costume room for some Broadway play about white water and we're the chorus line. We are all told to keep our feet up if we fall out of the raft (foot entrapment being the number one danger in white water). I look around the room. I'm proud of these college students who probably all stayed up until 2 A.M. the night before.

At the back of the gear room, John Pilley stands with Dave Perrin, one of our guides for the day and the manager of the NOC Chattooga Outpost. Dave graduated with me from Wofford in 1977 and Pilley taught him how to paddle. Dave's just-gone gray hair is a complement to Pilley's faded almost white. Tufts of Pilley's hair stick out from under a winter hat he plans to wear under his helmet. Dave and Pilley look like they are cut from the same rough cloth, both compact and strong, both comfortable in their clothes. Pilley's already dressed in his ancient wet suit. Dave wears Carhartt work pants and a fleece that looks like it could have been bought a decade ago. Dave still calls Pilley "Doc" and shares the same deep affection we all do for the Chattooga old-timer. In several phone conversations Dave has expressed regret that he hasn't seen Pilley more in the past few years and is looking forward to guiding him down the river.

Rafting is not something Pilley has ever cared for. He has always seen it as a recreational activity that doesn't require a high enough skill level to make it worthwhile. Pilley always resisted encouraging Wofford students to experience rivers in rafts and never allowed for organized raft trips to become part of the Wofford Outdoors program, though raft trips would have brought in many more students than the "hard boating skills" Pilley preferred. Over twenty-five years, a hundred or so Wofford students experienced the Chattooga with Pilley, and several dozen even advanced far enough in their skills to descend the section we would experience today. Dave had been among that elite group that Pilley had once led down Section IV, as later, I had. Now that Pilley is in his seventies, Section III is a little more his speed. In his fourth decade paddling the Chattooga, he's finally growing a little wary of Section IV's difficulties, and when I kid him about the rafts he explains that a raft trip with my class and Dave Perrin is looking pretty good.

Dave went to work for NOC shortly after he graduated from college and in a few years was running this outpost, the most romantic assignment in NOC's paddling empire. The mystique associated with the Chattooga Outpost rises from its isolation but also, maybe, from the sense of danger associated with the river. On a free-flowing stream, the guides don't know what to expect day to day. They need to be familiar with the river and adjust their guiding to actual river conditions, not some idea of what the river was like yesterday or last week.

And as the safety video confirms, the Chattooga is a river with a history of danger—for both novices and experts. Eighteen people have died in white-water boating accidents below the Highway 76 bridge, many of them rafters. NOC has never lost a guest on the Chattooga, though one of its expert guides drowned on a raft trip in 1979 while kayaking along as a safety boat. It was a freak accident in the Five Falls area that shook the company deeply and confirmed an even greater emphasis on safety on all rivers.

The perception of risk has been good for business on the Chattooga. Commercial rafting offers guests a chance to see some wild country and experience some formidable rapids that would be unavailable to them as consumers without advances in the industrialization of river running—its technology and knowledge. In the thirty years since the founding of the Nantahala Outdoor Center, commercial rafting has grown from a fringe sport conducted by a few for a few to the largest industry in many of the rural mountain counties like the ones we're visiting. Almost one hundred thousand people visit the Chattooga each year to float it. Ninety percent of them pay a commercial raft company to take them down. All who sign up for the adventure sign waivers saying they understand that river running has risks.

NOC has operated quite successfully for thirty years with the Chattooga as a source of profit. Some would argue this industrialization of the river—running tourists down in large, inflatable rubber boats—is no different really than running logs down the Chattooga in 1910 or, more recently, towns like Cashiers or Clayton running raw sewage down in the 1960s. There's no doubt rafting is cleaner and has a lower impact on the watershed, but use of any sort alters many things. Aldo Leopold used to like to say that the first law of intelligent tinkering is not to throw away any of the pieces. On the Chattooga if anything has been thrown away, it is the idea of a low-use river corridor. There are many people with access to the corridor now.

Use has been managed. There is a cap on commercial but not private river use, and for the past decade use has leveled off or even entered a period of decline. Today's hot kayakers paddle the free-flowing Chattooga when it's up to an exciting level, but many prefer the park and play rivers like the dam-release Ocoee in eastern Tennessee with roadside hydraulics, or play holes, where they can practice their rodeo moves. Who knows if commercial rafting will even survive on the Chattooga? How much can production and consumption drop in an industry before it's driven into extinction? From 1998 until 2002, four years of drought did its part in limiting the excitement, as has the South Carolina and Georgia public schools' opening earlier and earlier in August. I'm sure my former employers are watching the numbers and the bottom line of the outpost each year as market conditions change.

The government has always been aware of the problems of overuse and has taken action to assure the quality of experience in this Wild and Scenic River corridor. The Forest Service regulates the rafting companies to ensure as little impact on the ecology of the river and its water quality as possible. Raft trips must launch at appointed intervals, so there's some need for dispatch in routing guests through the preliminaries—safety video, dressing, the bus ride to the put-in. "There must be some system in place to assure 150 people from three different raft companies don't arrive at scenic Five Falls at the same time on a busy Saturday," Dave explains when I ask him why things move on such a tight schedule.

Dickey's characters escaped from the city, from routine, hoping to leave their roles as consumers far behind. Their equipment was minimal. Their knowledge of the territory was limited to road maps and a few topos. Their skills were marginal. The risk was high. In Dickey's fictional world, they take the risk, and they all suffer.

Of course, I want something different for my students. I watch them line up to be fitted for PFDs, wet suits, and helmets, and I want them to be safe, though I do want them to feel the wildness Dickey and his friends encountered here in the 1960s and Rick Bass felt here in the 1980s. I hope that wildness hasn't retreated into some cave or hole in the river's bank. I know I want what educators have always wanted. I want the students to see, to experience, and most important to understand.

But understand what? If this raft trip is worth the price of admission, it will show the students that this river exists in some place other than books, though everyone has an opinion as to why it exists. Are there many Chattoogas or just one constantly being redefined by what people want from it? Asking always what a wild landscape can do for us was addressed by westerner, environmentalist, and novelist Wallace Stegner in a 1962 letter published as part of an Interior Department report: "We simply need the wild country available to us, even if we never do more than drive to its edge and look in. For it can be a means of reassuring ourselves of our sanity as creatures, a part of the geography of hope."

So what's in it for us? I ask as I look around at my newly armored wildness warriors. In some strange way it's my belief that contact with this river can extend Stegner's geography of hope eastward and the students will get it, and, getting it, they will want to keep the Chattooga wild and preserve more watery territory like it. If it takes these rubber rafts and helmets and PFDs to get them in contact with this little bit of wildness, then so be it.

On our way to the put-in, we see a black bear crossing Chattooga Ridge Road in front of the blue NOC school bus loaded with yellow rafts. I catch one black haunch, a little patch of wildness, as it disappears into pines on the roadside. Dave says, "That bear's been raiding my beehives," and I remember that Dave is not a tourist. This place of myth and controversy is his home, not simply some abstract geography of hope. For me the bear is a scrap of wildness; for Dave, a troublesome neighbor robbing him of honey.

Dave, his wife, and two children live in a log cabin he built on a small mountain several miles from the outpost. They've made a life here on the Chattooga, a life rooted and responsible to the land, the various communities, and each other. Last winter I called and drove over to talk to him about NOC, the river, and its history.

"Life at the outpost with our neighbors is quite complex, usually pleasant," Dave said. But in the past twenty years, NOC's truck has been stolen, and the guides have been "harassed and shot at." Dave told these stories, trying to explain the territory to me, as he sat next to his wood stove in the basement of his log house. "A man next door to the outpost was killed by his uncle's half-brothers. He lived in a trailer and dipped water out of the creek down there. Drugs and drinking. James Dickey didn't come and write about that."

I look around the bus as we drive Chattooga Ridge Road toward the put-in on Highway 76 and wonder what scenarios of violence and inbreeding might dance through the heads of these mostly suburban college students. Do they worry about the random act of violence? I ask Tiffany, cinched up tight in her personal flotation device, what she's worried about. Her face betrays her concern.

"Will I fall out?" That's Tiffany's only articulate fear at this point on the ride. Will the river reach up and snatch her down into the world of risk?

As the guides begin to unload the rafts from on top of the blue NOC bus, I realize we have a high percentage of female guides on this trip. There are two women guiding rafts, Heather and Ann, plus the safety boater, a blonde named Lauren, a woman Dave says has been a kayak instructor and guide at the outpost for ten years. This stands in stark contrast to the "testosterone river" that I've come to expect. Dave says that it's partly due to this late-season trip and the luck of the draw—these three women are now a large percentage of those who still remain at the outpost now that high season is long gone.

Heather, the trip leader, wears a black helmet with a long beak in the back, like a thick bird's turned around backward. We listen as she leads us through our round of chores to prepare for launching: after assignment of personnel (six people in most boats), each group hauls boats, paddles, and safety gear down the winding asphalt ramp past the bathrooms and changing rooms.

Heather instructs us to apply a last snugness check of PFDs. I notice that Tiffany gets another student to pull up on her shoulders and, sure enough, the jacket stays put. My colleague biology professor Ellen Goldey clicks away with a digital camera, documenting our launch for the class Web site. Thomas and Amelia, two students who have experience with rafting, sit on the large side tubes of Ann's raft, ready to launch. I join Tiffany and them. The other students fan out among the four other rafts. Pilley, Dave, and Terry Ferguson, our geologist for a day, enter a smaller raft and float out into the current with Dave in the rear.

We push off into the current and drift a little until we're away from shore. Ann has long blond hair pulled into a ponytail under her blue helmet. She sits on the raft's black tube and leans out to sink her canoe paddle deep in the current. She's outfitted for action: climbing carabiners looped through the straps of her PFD, and there's a safety whistle hanging from a clip. Like most of us, she's wearing river sandals, but her feet are bare, wearing no thick socks against the chill of October water.

Ann goes through the river guide's drill: "Okay, when I say paddle forward, everybody paddle." We follow her lead and the raft surges into the flow. "Now, all back," Ann says, and we reverse our stroke. "And finally, if I ask for a right or left draw, you do this," she says as she places her paddle far out and pulls back toward the boat.

I look back over my shoulder and watch as everyone launches, boat by boat, into the Chattooga's green current. We're out far enough in the river so that I can almost see Bull Sluice two hundred yards upstream. Between the put-in beach and huge infamous rapid, there are rounded boulders and broken beards of white water where the river drops over cobbles and ledges. In the other direction, beyond the ruins of the old steel bridge and the new concrete Highway 76 bridge, the river looks calm, with little to warn us of what waits downstream.

"The ordeal ahead," an early guidebook calls the approach to Section IV. Maybe it remains so. I watch my fifteen students, colleagues, and old friends smiling in anticipation as they paddle their boats one by one into the easy access of the Chattooga's swift current. It's so simple and egalitarian: Pay your seventy-five dollars, strap on a PFD and helmet, listen to a safety talk, and venture into your own little adventure. "Let them tell their story," Dave Perrin reminded me when I asked what he thought I should write about the worth of a rafting adventure. "These are the guests and it's how they feel that matters."

I glance around the raft. Tiffany's here in the boat with me, and it's obvious she's loving it. She's not exactly smiling, but her eyes are wide open and she's gripping hard on the paddle shaft. She's highly aware that something wild is waiting downstream.

Maybe Pilley was right when he demanded that we all learn to paddle our own boats if we were to venture below the bridge, but looking at Tiffany's anticipation is a good argument for the easy access of rafting. One hundred thousand Tiffanys a year see the river from the tube of a raft. Do they really see the river? Is their appreciation of water, sky, and riverbank as deep as that of a kayaker or a canoeist? I can't answer such questions, especially with Ann calling for "all forward" so we can catch up with the trip headed downstream.

It's sunny when we get out from shore. The trip is underway. The students chatter among themselves. Ann answers a few questions from Tiffany, Amelia, and Thomas. She's a Davidson College graduate, a history major, and, no, she doesn't know exactly what she'll do when she "grows up." As we float along, the incessant pull of the river is downward; we're rolling along on a tilting surface spangled with exploding stars. Before I know it, we've tumbled through Surfing Rapid, Screaming Left Turn, Rock Jumble, and we're approaching Woodall Shoals. The pace is much quicker than kayaking. In the raft things move fast, but the power of each rapid is diminished by the multiple paddlers.

We head for the cheat chute on Woodall Shoals, and raft by raft we tumble past the killer hole. Ann points back upstream at the water circulating back toward the ledge. "That doesn't look so bad," Thomas says. "Let's go back up and shoot it." Tiffany glances back up toward the murderous, churning water. "I think we'll stay here," Ann says, noticing Tiffany's concern.

Below Woodall Shoals the river's character changes. Seven Foot Falls is the first place where the guides set serious safety ropes on Section IV, the lead guide eddying his raft above the drop and hopping out onto the rocks with a coiled yellow rope in case someone falls out. When positioned, he holds up the rope. A raft peels out and heads for a horizon line and disappears. A guide wearing a fireman's helmet and levering the boat right with the paddle is the last thing I see.

We sit and wait for a signal to proceed. Downstream, Seven Foot is one of those scenic spots where the river constricts to nothing. It looks as if the Chattooga disappears through a single watery slot between gray boulders. White pines bend down sharply over the current like some sumi painting. The banks rise sharply from river to ridge.

One by one, the other four rafts peel out from the eddy above Seven Foot Falls and proceed after they receive the green light. Ann's boat takes up the rear. By the time we approach, commit, and disappear into Seven Foot, everyone else is waiting in the eddy below. In a raft the drop feels more violent than in a kayak. In a kayak the approach to Seven Foot is endless and then it simply happens: the bottom falls out and the water directs you downward. The first time I ran it I flipped on the approach in a little wave. Upside down, I gathered myself, set up to roll, and popped upright just as my bow slipped over the lip of the falls. Nothing has ever equaled that first time. This time, as a raft tumbles over the brink, rubber folds upon rubber, mass shifts, gear scatters, and then at the bottom it somehow all sorts itself out amid laughter, relief, and paddle slaps. This is the essence of rafting—the communal victory—and even a hardcore kayaker like me feels the draw of it. "Team Wofford," someone says in the lead raft and there's one more paddle slap before we head downstream.

A half mile below Seven Foot we pass Stekoa Creek joining the Chattooga from the Georgia side. Stekoa Creek is one of the largest tributaries of the river, draining the valley to the northwest that the town of Clayton sprawls through. It's been several days since a major rain, but I can see the sediment-stained run-off from construction and development upstream. Stekoa Creek causes one of the biggest threats to the Chattooga. Its influence is great enough to shift the designation of the river from Wild and Scenic upstream to simply Scenic below the creek's confluence. "We've got little green cards back at the outpost," Ann says as we float past. "Be sure to fill them out before you leave. Your concern about Stekoa will help protect the watershed."

The river picks up intensity just below Stekoa Creek with long rolling Class III shoals. We stay far left and run aground several times in the shallow spots.

We beach the rafts just downstream on the South Carolina side, and the students and guides hike fifty yards to Long Creek Falls, a scenic, three-stage thirty-foot cascade just out of sight. "Guests have to wear PFDs and helmets," Ann reminds the three students from my raft as they depart for the waterfall. After the students are safely dispatched to the base of the falls, Ann wanders over to chat with the other guides. I sit on the raft's thwart and catch up on my notes now that we have a moment of calmness off the river.

As I wait for the students to reappear from the falls, I begin to think about Dickey and *Deliverance* and how Dave says that the movie never really died out up here. "For about eight years you didn't hear about it," he said when we talked at his house earlier. "Now Ted Turner reruns it three or four times a year on TBS. Occasionally you still get the yahoo who likes to squeal."

We load up and head downstream. Long Creek Falls is finally fully visible as we drift past, a beauty spot among many others, tucked just back from the river. "Waterfall country," that's what one friend calls the Chattooga. There's something about a waterfall that digs deep in the psyche. Maybe it's the sound. Some say it's the way the falling water stirs the air. Whatever the reason, I'm drawn to them. So is everyone else.

Downstream from Long Creek Falls a huge boulder appears to block the whole river—Deliverance Rock. Here several scenes were shot for the film. We pull up next to Terry's raft and catch him in the midst of a geology lecture concerning the boulder. He points out that the slab is tilted downstream. "Notice that this is the angle of repose of most of the boulders in the stream." I see what he means and think back to Terry's backpack tumbling down the mountain. Upon close inspection it's clear that this boulder has in the past broken loose from the gorge wall, tumbled into the river, and at some point done a barrel roll to end up in its present position. What could possibly move a rock of this size? "Deliverance Rock was tossed by the current in a giant flood at some point," he says, pointing out the way the boulder rests in the streambed.

Just downstream from Deliverance Rock, Raven's Cliff rises into view. One of the most impressive geologic formations on the entire Chattooga, its flinty presence has always been a gateway, a portal into the deepest wildness the river can offer. The overhanging cliff with horizontal banding forms what looks like the beak and eye of a raven when looked at from below. The heavy beak of the raven points downstream toward what's to come—the gorge of the Five Falls.

It's here, just upstream of the six-foot ledge and Class IV rapid shadowed by the dark, imposing cliffs, where we'll have lunch. In late May of 1999 a young Pennsylvania hiker, Rachel Trois, forded the river with a group of friends and lost her footing and was swept downstream. She drowned and her body became lodged in rocks at the turbulent base of the rapids. The futile efforts to recover her body were, according to press reports, "the most massive ever undertaken by the people in the mountain towns along the river."

Over a month passed, but all efforts to recover her body failed. The construction of a portable temporary five-foot dam was unsuccessful and led to weeks of skirmishes among environmentalists, rescue workers, and politicians. It's eerie to think of the rafting companies running their trips throughout the ordeal. The rafts passed over the very spot Rachel was pinned by the powerful currents and snagged on debris.

What was at issue in the recovery of Rachel's body was whether the grieving family had the legal right to hire a company to install the dam that could possibly divert this Wild and Scenic River long enough to perform the recovery. Environmentalists argued that the construction of the portable dam, which required boring holes in the bedrock on the river's bottom, potentially damaged the river, compromised the integrity of the Wild and Scenic Rivers Act, and opened the river to other forms of unlawful use—such as the road that was built into the remote stretch of river to facilitate the prolonged, ill-timed recovery effort.

When Senator Strom Thurmond, then the ninety-eight-year-old senior senator from South Carolina, became involved in the controversy, the complexity doubled and turned political. One of the issues in the recovery case was the safety of the workers installing the dam. Environmentalists and some locals who had years of experience recovering bodies from the Chattooga (Rachel was the thirty-sixth since 1970) felt that the "rescue" should only be attempted if the river was down to an acceptable level—1.1 to 0.8 feet deep. During the entire period of the tragedy the Chattooga ran at least 1.7 feet deep, a pushy level on narrow Section IV.

Because of safety concerns, many opposed the continued effort by the New Jersey dam company that had offered their services free to the family to install a series of dams to assist in recovery. "Of course I feel for the family and wish we could get her out," Buzz Williams said in July, almost six weeks after the drowning. "The Forest Service got out of the way [for Thurmond] and this monster got out of control."

The monster Buzz referred to was partially Senator Thurmond's threat to introduce legislation to restrict access to commercial rafting if the river was proven to be dangerous. The river *is* dangerous. There is nothing to prove. A grieving father's unprecedented effort to recover his lost daughter is only one in an endless line of tragedies that haunt the banks of the Chattooga.

Rachel's story grabbed the interest of the national press, including CNN, the *Washington Post*, and the *New York Times*, and still today stands as an important watermark in the evolving use of the Chattooga. Rachel's body was never pulled from the river. As the family grieved, a few human bones swept clean by the current were pulled from the pool below Raven's Shoot—the only remains of Rachel ever recovered.

Soon it's lunchtime and ahead of us we see the rugged rock ledge jutting from the South Carolina side where we'll stop and eat. Above us looms the raven. It's sunny and warm, with the sun directly above. The river is an audible presence, dropping over Raven's Cliff ledge, which is just upstream from our destination. Before we stop for lunch we'll run the rafts down one by one through Raven's Shoot, passing near Rachel's final resting place. The rapid is a river-wide ledge, and in a kayak it's quite a formidable drop. Maybe it's something about the spot—the cliff, the sound of the water, the sense of what's downstream—but Raven's Shoot has always seemed difficult on my solo efforts.

The water funnels down a diagonal slide close on the South Carolina side. That's where we line up and run the rapid, and it's where most boats run it at normal water levels. The rafts make it seem easy, with lunchtime anticipation pushing us all through and over behind the lunch rock to unload.

The guides haven't said anything about Rachel's death, even though we pass near the hydraulic at the bottom of the rapid, and I decide to keep it to myself out of respect for the dead hiker. I paddle on in spite of the historic battle that ensued on this spot. Bus companies don't tell tales of the worst auto wrecks, and airline pilots don't talk about crashes. It makes sense. A tragedy like Rachel's is the uncommon reality of the river. It feeds the myth.

The outfitter's lunch is spread out on a colorful blanket covering the warm rock, and all the guests wait to eat and drink their fill—students and faculty fanned out on the rock, guides clustered together in the shadow of the cliff. The students file past the blanket, followed by me, Ellen, Pilley, and Terry. We all munch our turkey on whole-wheat sandwiches, gobble gorp by the handfuls, follow it all with pickles, and end with a cookie or two, decimating the famous NOC lunch fare, all of which was carried downstream in five-gallon white pickle buckets snapped with climbing carabiners on the grab lines of the rafts.

Though it's difficult to get the students focused on "content" after turkey sandwiches and gorp, I gather them anyway. Terry's held off most of his geology lecturing until now, but he's ready to go. He steps to the end of the lunch rock and I introduce him, though everyone already knows who he is.

I realize that it's hard to grasp the depth of geologic time, especially during the time constraints of a one-day raft trip. I tell Terry the guides have given him fifteen minutes for his minilecture, "and then it's time to head for Five Falls."

Terry jokes that he only has to cover a billion years and pulls out a topo map of this lower section of the Chattooga and passes it around.

"What do you see? What does the river do?" We look at the map as it travels among us. I think I see what he's getting at. The river comes out of the mountains heading hard and straight almost due south, then a few miles below the Five Falls area it takes a turn and heads southeast.

"Takes a hard left turn," one student says.

"The Chattooga's headwaters used to be part of the headwaters of the Chattahoochee, the river that runs through Atlanta. The Chattahoochee drains into the Gulf of Mexico," Terry explains in his professor lecture voice, holding up the map. "The Savannah captured the Chattooga and now it's part of the Atlantic drainage."

Terry then launches into a ten-minute lecture illustrated by line drawings on a portable marker board. "Like most epic stories, this one begins in the middle; for almost half a billion years an ocean known as the Iapetus existed where the Atlantic is today. Very gradually around 500 million years ago, two continents that would later become North America and Africa crept toward each other at about the rate fingernails grow." As we listen he talks about this collision of continents and how it took place over the next 250 million years "as convective forces in the earth's mantle pushed the continents together like a garbage compactor."

Instead of a week's garbage, Terry explains, what disappeared, slowly pulled down and melted deep within the earth in the big crunch, was most of the floor of a huge ocean basin between the continents. "As the continents and sediments of the ocean basin came together, the rocks of the continents slowly downwarped and crumpled under great temperature and pressure," he says, taking the map, which has returned to him, and pushing it at both ends. "The rocks were also pushed upward and mountains rose—the Appalachians. By 350 million years ago a jagged range of peaks more like the Himalayas than our present-day Blue Ridge had risen out of what is now eastern North America."

Terry's feeling it, the big story; his voice booms louder, trying to drown out the rapid working at his feet. I look around. Do the students get it? Is this lecture in situ working? Is this better than an indoor classroom?

"By 250 million years ago the building of the Appalachians was over. To the east of these mountains stretched the vast continent of Africa. The oceans existed only to the west. Up from these oceans, rivers and streams eroding headward had cut into the mountains. The running water of rivers and streams is as old as the rocks they wear away. Rivers and rocks have been around longer than life has existed on the Earth." Then he describes rock and rain as dance partners that have existed "as long as gravity has worked its magic." Terry points back over his shoulder at the staircase of rapids and waterfalls slowly cutting their way back further and further into the mountains—"Nature's great grinding machines."

Then, for me at least, the excitement of geologic time deepens as Terry inches closer to the present: "These older rivers and streams worked the land for over 150 million years until around 200 million years ago when the great convective conveyor belt beneath the crust of the Earth reversed and the connected continents began to slowly break apart in a great rift. Moving at a rate of inches a year, the rift grew and eventually filled with water—the beginning of the Atlantic Ocean. After 200 million years Africa and North America continue to move apart and the Atlantic grows ever wider.

"When the Atlantic formed, new rivers and streams began to cut rapidly from the coast into the mountains from the east, like gullies cutting across an untended farm field in a summer thunderstorm," exclaims Terry. "The forces were in place for the great war to level and drain the high country, the combatants were the young Atlantic rivers and the older rivers of the Gulf.

"The older rivers and streams flowing west and south out of the mountains toward the Gulf of Mexico had settled into maturity. Many of the river valleys were wide and filled with the sediment of ages. These Gulf rivers—the Tennessee, the French Broad, the New, and the Chattahoochee—had settled in to their work of erosion, deposition, and transportation of sediment with slow certainty flowing down gently sloping surfaces. These Gulf rivers have a much longer journey to the sea than their opponents to the east. Many flow over ten times as far to reach the ocean as those that flow to the Atlantic.

"The new youthful rivers cutting back from the Atlantic were much more efficient and effective at cutting deep V-shaped valleys with steeper gradients," Terry says, "like the river you see behind me. Over the past 175 million years they have efficiently leveled the mountains that once rose over the southeastern piedmont and transported and deposited a thick wedge of sediment over the coastal plain.

"Geologists use the language of warfare to describe what happens when 'youthful' rivers cut quickly (in geologic time) across the headwaters of the older, less efficient streams and take over their drainages: *stream piracy, capture,* and *beheading.*" He holds up his portable marker board and draws a picture of the Chattooga—a line with a long downward curve cut by a perpendicular line from the right (the Savannah). "It's what happened here," Terry says again as we look downstream. "The Chattahoochee's headwaters—in this case the Chattooga—were captured by the younger Savannah. If you wanted to you could say some pirates came up the Savannah and cut off the head of the Chattahoochee." The students laugh and nod.

Back in the rafts, we head downstream. The next mile and a half is what's known as the calm before the storm, a stretch of easy water. We bump over a few ledges and ripples but encounter no major rapids. Of course, Five Falls is the storm, focusing all our anticipation as we approach it. Five Falls is the highlight on any Section IV trip. It's the big roller coaster in the amusement park of the Chattooga, the exclamation mark on the wild sentence this isolated river utters.

A quarter mile above Five Falls Dave paddles up beside the raft to point out Camp Creek's confluence with the Chattooga. It's here he says that the burial scene after the rape in *Deliverance* was filmed.

"If you go in there in the heat of the summer it's like walking into a grown-over grotto."

The beauty of the spot comes through clearly in the film. After the rape the four adventurers drag the dead body of the rapist through ferns and over rocks. Around them is bird song and the sound of falling water. They squat in the rich forest soil and grub the grave out with their bare hands. From the raft the little creek looks like a dozen others on the river. There are no plaques to acknowledge that this spot has been certified by Hollywood, and the guides don't say anything as we float past.

Christopher Dickey reports in *Summer of Deliverance* that the script called this "dark laurel thicket" "Resting Place." There were several days of shooting at Resting Place, but the afternoon the rape scene was shot, even the studio photographer was excluded from the set. Only the participating actors and the film crew were allowed into the dark clearing. Burt Reynolds and Ronny Cox weren't even there. The only actors present were Ned Beatty, playing the rape victim; Jon Voight; and Bill McKinney, a Hollywood character actor, and Herbert "Cowboy" Coward, an actor in a western amusement park in the Smokies, playing the rapists.

Now Resting Place rests only in the memory of the *Deliverance* crew and a few hundred like Dave who know of its use as a set. The place is now just another beautiful little intersection of mountain stream and river, a small confluence. But what lingers there? What residue remains of the filming? Human use could alter the atmosphere around a place, and maybe story hallows the ground. As we float past I listen to the lapping river and birdsong and hope to hear voices, the ghosts of the Chattooga's human past.

Soon after Camp Creek, Ann prepares us for what's to come, explaining how Five Falls is a quarter mile of some of the fiercest commercially rafted white water in the country and how we'll drop seventy-five feet through five difficult rapids—Entrance, Corkscrew, Crack-in-the-Rock, Jawbone, and Sock-em-Dog—in short order. In the gorge below us, the currents swirl and convulse through narrow chutes. There is little chance for recovery if we spill. On several of the rapids she will call for us to "set" as we plunge over the drop. The turbulence, she explains, could toss us around and the safest spot is the bottom of the raft. She demonstrates, dropping to her knees with her paddle folded beside her. "When I say, 'set,' I want you all to squat in the center of the raft," she says, once more going through the motion. We all attempt to set, folding into the middle of the slowly drifting raft afloat on the easy water. I glance around. Tiffany looks concerned. Her anxiety about white water has surfaced again. She grips her paddle, and her focus narrows to the two inches in front of her face. It's the opposite of the thousand-mile stare you hear about with combat veterans. This gaze you see on the face of novice rafters is inward focused, a self-searching stare into the depths.

I remember clearly how terrible an ordeal that first trip through Five Falls can become. My first time through the gorge I was with John Pilley. I'd already flipped at the top of Seven Foot Falls, and so I wasn't feeling especially confident.

That day he led me through the set-up for Entrance Rapid, and I followed. I flipped in Entrance and set up to roll in the pool at the bottom. I missed my roll and kept trying over and over. Pilley was beside me, but we were drifting toward Corkscrew, one of the most difficult of the Five Falls. I was hanging in my boat, still trying to roll, but tiring quickly, with no success righting myself. "Your spray skirt has popped," Pilley yelled, paddling up beside me. Out of instinct, I reached out and grabbed Pilley's boat as the two of us drifted toward the approach to Corkscrew. Pilley looked down at my hand holding his grab loop. "Lane, let go of my boat," Pilley said. "You're on your own."

I let go and Pilley swiftly disappeared down the rapid. I flushed through Corkscrew's atomic flume—a terrible feeling, tossing and banging and sliding through the Chattooga's famous spin cycle. The only thing to be said for swimming Corkscrew is, if you're lucky and avoid the two major offset hydraulics, it's over fast. This time I was lucky. At the bottom Pilley was waiting to pull me over. A rope hit me in the head and I grabbed on and a friendly kayaker tugged me to shore.

I know that Ann's skill and the NOC's experience make it highly unlikely that any of us will swim Corkscrew. I wish I could assure Tiffany through tables and charts that her trip through Five Falls is most likely going to be uneventful but charged with excitement. I can see little of that assurance on her face now as Ann rudders us into an eddy on the South Carolina shore and points downstream. "That's Entrance Rapid," she says, pointing out the boulder-strewn route the first raft is negotiating below us. "Danny's headed down first to set safety at the bottom," she says.

Soon the signal comes from below. Ann tells us all to paddle forward and we quickly slip past boulders and through small waves on the approach to Entrance Rapid. The approach is long and technical as Ann rudders the raft past boulders and through narrow chutes and we approach the drop on the Georgia side of the river. Quickly and violently we're in it, the first of the Five Falls, as we slide between the shore and a huge boulder. No one falls out and Ann eddies us in the small recovery pool I had unsuccessfully tried my roll in several decades before. I look downstream and I can see the jagged entryway to Corkscrew. I point out the next rapid to my students, all slapping paddles after the successful run, but no one is paying me any attention. They're caught in the moment, and rightly so.

When Ann gets the signal we drift forward and drop down into Corkscrew, which quickly catches us and begins to convulse around us as we ride it through to the bottom—currents going left and right, water forced in contrary directions, rocks sluiced endlessly by the force and power of the full Chattooga. Ann keeps us far left of the big hole that flips so many kayaks. We paddle forward and gain tremendous speed. All's a wet blur as the raft fills to overflow. At the bottom of the rapid I glance up and we roll past the guides with ropes standing on rocks to our right. They hold their yellow ropes chest high and acknowledge our passage.

We eddy out in the pool at the bottom. I remember that it's here that my heart generally starts again when I'm in my kayak. What's above is the place on the Chattooga where real power unfolds—the power of a wild river twisting through broken boulders and resistant bedrock. I always stop here and reflect on that power and thank the river gods for my safe passage.

Ann gets us all out of the raft on the left bank, and we work our way downstream over boulders. We'll portage Crack-in-the-Rock, and the guides will work the empty rafts down through the river-wide ledge for safety. The ledge looks harmless compared to what we've experienced so far, but each of the three "cracks" has its potential nightmares. The right crack is the widest. For years it had the trunk of a tree lodged in the middle of it, but there was just enough room on each side for a kayak, canoe, or even a small raft to pass. Some flood dislodged the log and now the route is clear, but a grabby hydraulic forms at the bottom of the five-foot ledge. The middle crack is three-feet wide and is the preferred route now by kayakers at most water levels. We watch as one of NOC's safety boats slips through with paddle turned sideways.

Left Crack is avoided at all costs, though the unlucky do end up there. Occasionally paddlers capsize in Corkscrew and drift through the recovery pool at the rapid's bottom and flush through the left crack. The narrow passage of Left Crack is shaped like an hour-glass, and numerous deaths have occurred here, some where the bodies were not recovered for weeks.

Our guides slip the empty rafts through the narrow opening of Left Crack with lines, then reenter the boats at the bottom. We stand waiting on gray boulders along the shore and then reenter the stream as well. Next up is Jawbone with its powerful flow, eddy-hopping, offset ledge, and famous hazard called Hydroelectric Rock, a huge undercut center-stream boulder with a dangerous passage underneath from front to back. Paddlers out of their boats have flushed through this suckhole. Some say even boats have been sucked through the hole.

Our approach is a little off, and we come into the eddy above the ledge with too much speed and end up slamming into a large boulder. We spin around and twist backward and head downstream. "Set," Ann screams as we slip backward over the ledge. We're all in the middle of the boat on our knees. The rocks scrape across my kneecaps and I look up to see the world passing in reverse. I see where in 1979 an NOC safety boater slipped out of a small eddy backward and was pinned beneath the undercut rock. His kayak broke in half, and the current ripped off his helmet and PFD. It took five hours to recover his body. It's not a pleasant observation to make while you are spinning backward through Jawbone. But Ann's in control, though working from the wrong end of the raft. Soon Hydro slips past and Ann reaches for calm water and pulls us into the small pool below the rapid.

In the eddy another guide secures the boat, one foot on a boulder and another on the raft's tube. More paddle slapping. Ann laughs at our backward passage and says we're lucky and everybody did a good job on the set.

Resting in the eddy, I look back upstream and see that in the next raft the guide is missing. He's somehow fallen out. My students are riding through Jawbone guideless! They don't know it since everyone is looking downstream. They sit passively with their paddles in the air as they tumble and shift down Jawbone's ledge. Looking around I see that the other guides are already aware and are rock-hopping to get into position to help. I see the guide's feet and helmeted head bobbing down right behind the guests, but too far away to be of any use to the run-away raft.

As the raft passes a finger of boulders, another guide hops onto the boat's stern and grabs the absent guide's paddle and plants a hard stroke to steer the runaway raft toward the left shore. This stops the forward progress toward Sock-em-Dog. The lost guide is recovered upstream, and I don't think any of the students have noticed yet.

Everybody laughs and we regroup for the final drop of Five Falls—the infamous Sock-em-Dog, a true Class V with a hydraulic at the bottom deep enough to swallow a canoe.

Sometime in the late fifties, on Hugh Caldwell's descent of Section IV, the group was in fifteen-foot shoe-keeled Grummans. They portaged Woodall Shoals and many of the drops in the Five Falls. They decided to run Jawbone. Caldwell worked his way downstream to photograph Fritz Orr Jr. running the rapid, but all that came through was Orr's canoe, upside down. Orr survived and was rescued upstream. Caldwell scrambled over large boulders to catch the canoe in the eddy after it had come over Sock-em-Dog. When he reached the pool there was no canoe. In a half hour of searching, all they found was a canteen that had been tied to a thwart. At dark they gave up on the lost canoe. The next day they came back with grappling irons tied to ropes and probed the hole at Sock-em-Dog's bottom, but never found any trace of the lost boat.

I like to think it's still down there somewhere, the Chattooga's own *Titanic* sunk deep in the mystery. I know that's probably impossible, but it's still fun to imagine as we peel out and approach the seven-foot ledge with the monster hole at the bottom.

"Set," Ann screams as we fly off the launching pad, the jutting slab of rock boats use to get some lift to propel them over the worst of the hole. We land and power forward through the backwash. We've made it. Our boat will not join Fritz Orr Jr.'s ghost Grumman at the bottom of the river, a sort of river version of Davy Jones's locker.

After we recover at the bottom of Sock-em-Dog, we spin and slip through the hard-right turn of Shoulderbone, the last big rapid on the river. It's just like the guys in *Deliverance*, coming out of the river into the lake: "The bed-rocks fell away; another curve, one without rapids, began to open in front of us a hundred yards further on."

As we leave the current behind, I'm thinking about the significance of a living river's disappearance. The bow of the raft slips into the slack water of Lake Tugaloo, "the world's largest molasses impoundment," as humorist William Nealy called it in *Whitewater Home Companion*. It's like we've crossed the line between two worlds—movement and stillness, fast and slow, life and death.

This lake with the river channel now silted in below us is a perfect metaphor for our relationship to the myth of the Chattooga. The real river now runs somewhere down there below all our expectations, dreams, stories, fears. We must trust it's there, though we float always somewhere above it. It's like Thoreau's pond. "Let us settle ourselves," he says in *Walden,* "and work and wedge our feet downward through the mud and slush of opinion, and prejudice, and tradition, and delusion, and appearance."

In the old days the two-mile paddle across the lake was enough to dampen the spirits of all but the most dedicated.

Today, rather than asking tired, wet guests to stroke heavy rafts across the lake's calm expanse like a Viking raiding party, the three raft companies have pooled resources and hired a motorboat to shorten the journey. Ann explains to everyone how we'll clip the boats together and push the flotilla across the lake. She says the boat will come into view in only a few minutes. As a river guide, Ann's never known anything else but the motorboat, so she can't miss the old ways I'm left to consider.

Surely there's some advantage to stroking your own boat across the lake at the end of the run, but I can't articulate what it might be for the life of me. Payson Kennedy, in the Chattooga outpost's early years, believed deeply in the advantage of slowing down, doing things by hand. The guides pumped every raft up by hand and dug footings with shovels, foregoing the backhoe's easy trenching, and accrued some spiritual advantage by working with human muscle. There were many back then in the early seventies willing to follow Payson while working for NOC, the place "where work and play are one."

That early ethic has now faded some from company practice, and even the last great Chattooga ritual, crossing the great lake of molasses, has been given over to customer demand and the labor-saving concession of a two-stroke outboard.

I take one last paddle stroke and then I see the motorboat waiting low in the water along the shore just past where the river disappears. The boy they've hired to haul us home is smoking a cigarette as he waits. A thin plume of washed-out smoke knives toward the blue dome of heaven. He's wearing a cap, and he could just as easily be a bass fisherman stopped to take a leak, but no, Ann points ashore. "There's the boat," she says. "It won't be long now." As if waiting for her signal, the boy jerks the motor to life and the boat slices toward us.

They say that near the end of Dickey's life he worried about his responsibility for what had happened up here, for the changes that adventure seekers had brought to the mountains. I've always thought it was the deaths that haunted Dickey, the dozens of men, women, and children who have died embracing the wildness of the Chattooga that made Dickey reconsider his relationship to this place. How do we live in the face of such beauty, such raw power, what Dickey called near the bitter end of *Deliverance* "the true weight and purpose of all water"? That question is not easily answered. In order to answer it I would have to consider the whole range of pilgrims I have encountered along the Chattooga: Buzz, with his pure devotion for preservation and restoration of the watershed; Kyle Burrell, with his easy intimacy with the wild places upstream; Tiffany, with her guarded beginner's approach; and Dave Perrin, with his belief that the Chattooga is "the public's river" and should be enjoyed by all.

The myth of the Chattooga includes escape and relief. We've all experienced that here today. Separation. Initiation. Return. When we left the Highway 76 bridge behind, everyone knew odds were that we'd come out on the other end, but what the adventure promised was that we'd be alone with our thoughts and the river for a few hours. We'd get very wet and a little scared. We'd pull our chairs up to a feast of wildness and mystery like no other in the southeast.

Pilley is shivering in the raft next to me. The sun declines over the ridges to the west. The cool fall air has penetrated his wet suit, and it looks as if he's ready to get off the river. I'm glad I got down the river with him one more time before he someday soon decides to stay on calmer water.

The motorboat slips behind Heather's raft. Quickly the guides clip us all together using carabiners and the grab ropes on the rafts' sides. Soon we're underway, the rafts gathered into an out-of-shape flotilla pushed by a powerboat. From shore we must look like some engineer's jerry-rigged dream of movement over water. We must be quite a contrast to the sleek elegance of kayaks and canoes.

The guides take off their armor. Plastic paddles disappear into the bottom of the rafts. My students lean back on the inflated tubes and laugh and talk above the whining of the motor. The take-out is two miles down the lake. We're headed home to dry clothes and familiar territory.

There is not another long personal narrative in print that focuses on the Chattooga, though the river has been explored through personal narratives by some writers, including William Bartram, Rick Bass, and Christopher Camuto. Both Camuto's *Another Country: Journeying toward the Cherokee Mountains* and *A Fly Fisherman's Blue Ridge* contributed to this narrative in spirit and substance. I'd hope Camuto's beautiful prose instructed me on how to write at least "a few good sentences" in this work. Rick Bass will always be an inspiration for his heroic defense of his Montana home, the Yaak, and for his passionate prose about that wild landscape. His early experiences with the Chattooga, found in *Wild to the Heart*, made me focus on what could be said about this southern remnant wilderness.

Many texts and documents also informed my understanding of the human and the natural history of the Chattooga watershed. James Dickey's *Deliverance* stands like a cliff behind this work. Dickey's poems, his *Self-Interviews*, and *Nighthurdling* also contributed ideas, connections, and insights. John Boorman's film *Deliverance*, of course, was also central. Christopher Dickey's *Summer of Deliverance* contributed to my understanding of his father's relationship to the wild South, as did Henry Hart's biography, *James Dickey: The World as a Lie*. I carefully read several early chapters in Donald Greiner's *Women Enter the Wilderness*, parts of Ernest Suarez's *James Dickey and the Politics of Canon*, and several essays on *Deliverance* in *Struggling for Wings: The Art of James Dickey*, edited by Robert Kirschten. This list of Dickey criticism should by no means be mistaken as a review of the literature. There are many insights into the subject to be found in other notable scholarly work.

Sound Wormy: Memoir of Andrew Gennett, Lumberman, edited by Nicole Hayler, was helpful in understanding the historical forces that shaped the watershed. *The Chattooga: Wild and Scenic River* by Brian Boyd and *A Guide to the Chattooga River* by Butch Clay each contributed grounding in basic logistics and description as I made my way downstream. Both of these slim volumes are essential for exploring the watershed.

A Naturalist's Guide to the Southern Blue Ridge Front by L. L. Gaddy and *Carolina Rocks! The Geology of South Carolina* by Carolyn Hanna Murphy both provided insight into the natural history of the area. *The Mountain at the End of the Trail* by Robert Zahner and *Yesterday's Rabun* by Brian A. Boyd added understanding to the cultural history of the region.

There are many paddling guides with descriptions of the Chattooga's rapids and I consulted several of them—Randy Carter's *Canoeing White Water,* Bob Benner's *Carolina Whitewater,* and Gene Able and Jack Horan's *Paddling South Carolina* among them. The late William Nealy's cartoon map of the Chattooga Section III and IV in *Whitewater Home Companion* still stands as one of the best ways to navigate the river.

The *Chattooga Quarterly,* published by the Chattooga Conservancy, is a wealth of information. I read all of them cover to cover. Many thanks to Chattooga Conservancy for this, the finest introduction to the watershed.

Don Belt's *National Geographic* piece "White Water, Proud People" (April 1983) is one of the only extended pieces in the national press to explore the river, its people, and its history. The *Greenville News* published a series of articles on the tenth anniversary of the publication of Dickey's novel (1980) that remain one of the best sources of local responses to the river corridor; and through the years, *South Carolina Wildlife* has published a number of fine articles by Dot Jackson and others about the river and its people. *America Whitewater,* the journal of the American Whitewater Association, has also written extensively about paddling issues on the river through the years.

Payson Kennedy's article about first descents in the Southern Appalachians that appeared in John Lazenby's *First Descents* anthology from Menasha Ridge Press in the late 1980s added historic detail to the still incomplete story of the Chattooga's pioneers. Kennedy's archive of a few choice letters from Hugh Caldwell and Frank Bell is one of the most valuable resources available to any scholar of this river. Many thanks for giving me access to this treasure trove.

Finally though, *Chattooga* is first and foremost a book-length personal narrative. There is an environmental history of the Chattooga watershed yet to be done. This is not it. Let someone else paddle into that set of rapids. My personal experience with the watershed is at the center of this narrative. The "I" Henry David Thoreau talks about in *Walden* appears on the first page. Look to books such as Noah Adams's *Far Appalachia,* John Graves's *Goodbye to a River,* and Franklin Burroughs's *The River Home* if you want to understand why this river's story is told the way it is.

There is a great, unreported nature and culture of this river. I have launched into it. I hope that others with more patience for libraries will follow me down the river after this literary first descent.